GOD'S WORD FOR A JR. HIGH WORLD

Life at School

Kara Eckmann Powell

Gospel Light is an evangelical Christian publisher dedicated to serving the local church. We believe God's vision for Gospel Light is to provide church leaders with biblical, user-friendly materials that will help them evangelize, disciple and minister to children, youth and families.

We hope this Gospel Light resource will help you discover biblical truth for your own life and help you minister to youth. God bless you in your work.

For a free catalog of resources from Gospel Light please contact your Christian supplier or contact us at 1-800-4-GOSPEL *or* www.gospellight.com.

PUBLISHING STAFF
William T. Greig, Publisher
Dr. Elmer L. Towns, Senior Consulting Publisher
Dr. Gary S. Greig, Senior Consulting Editor
Pam Weston, Editor
Patti Pennington Virtue, Assistant Editor
Christi Goeser, Editorial Assistant
Kyle Duncan, Associate Publisher
Bayard Taylor, M.Div., Senior Editor, Theological and Biblical Issues
Kevin D. Parks, Cover Designer
Rosanne Richardson, Co-Cover Designer
Debi Thayer, Designer
Paul Fleischmann, Siv Ricketts and Natalie Chenault, Contributing Writers
ISBN 0-8307-2508-3

Printed in U.S.A.

You may make copies of portions of this book with a clean conscience if:

- you (or someone in your organization) are the original purchaser;
- you are using the copies you make for a noncommercial purpose (such as teaching or promoting your ministry) within your church or organization;
- you follow the instructions provided in this book.

However, it is ILLEGAL for you to make copies if:

- you are using the material to promote, advertise or sell a product or service other than for ministry fund-raising;
- you are using the material in or on a product for sale;
- you or your organization are **not** the original purchaser of this book.

By following these guidelines you help us keep our products affordable.
Thank you,
Gospel Light

Praise for Pulse

There is a cry from this generation for Truth. **Pulse** curriculum targets this cry by leading teenagers to the Truth. How exciting it is to have a curriculum that gives the depth through Scripture and fun through involvement. —**Helen Musick,** Youth Specialties National Resource Team member, national speaker and author

The **Pulse** curriculum is truly "cross-cultural." Built on the solid foundation of an understanding of junior highers' unique developmental needs and rapidly changing culture, it affords teachers and youth workers the opportunity to communicate God's unchanging Word to kids growing up in a world that increasingly muffles and muddles the truth. —**Walt Mueller,** President, Center for Parent/Youth Understanding and author of *Understanding Today's Youth Culture*

The creators and writers of this curriculum know and love young teens, and that's what sets good junior high curriculum apart from the mediocre stuff! —**Mark Oestreicher,** Vice President of Ministry Resources, Youth Specialties

Great biblical material, creative interaction and USER-FRIENDLY! What more could you ask? This stuff will help you see your junior highers reach their potential as disciples of Christ! I highly recommend it! —**Ken Davis,** President, Dynamic Communications International and award-winning author and speaker

It's about time that curriculum produced for junior highers took them and their youth workers seriously. **Pulse** does it and does it very well! This curriculum knows junior highers and proves that teens changed by Christ who are equipped and empowered by His Church really can change their world! I am planning to recommend **Pulse** enthusiastically to all my youth worker friends. —**Rich Van Pelt,** Strategic Relationships Director, Compassion International, author, speaker and veteran youth worker

I found **Pulse** to be a stimulating, engaging and spiritually challenging curriculum for middle school students. Kara Powell has developed a rich resource that provides teachers with strong content to teach and creative options to help teachers meet the individual needs of their students. Recognizing that spiritual formation is not an end in itself, **Pulse** provides a strategy for evangelism in each lesson that empowers students to share the gospel with their peers. This is a curriculum that makes genuine connections with middle school students and the culture in which they must live out their faith every day. —**Mark W. Cannister, Ed.D.,** Chair, Department of Youth Ministries, Gordon College

Written by veteran junior high youth workers who know how to communicate so kids will get the message! Kara has given youth workers a fresh tool that's user-friendly and geared to make a lasting impact by addressing the foundational issues of Christianity that sometimes take a backseat to trendy topical studies. —**Paul Fleischmann,** Executive Director, National Network of Youth Ministries

This is serious curriculum for junior highers! Not only does it take the great themes of the Christian faith seriously, but it takes junior highers seriously, as well. Young adolescents have a tremendous capacity for learning about spiritual things and this curriculum makes it possible for them to learn all they can about the God of the Bible—who loves them and wants to involve them *now* in His Church. This is the best I've seen yet. —**Wayne Rice,** author and Junior High Ministry Director, Understanding Your Teenager seminars

Life at School

CONTENTSCONTENTSCONTENTSCONTENTSCONTENTS

Contributors

Paul Fleischmann is the executive director and co-founder of the National Network of Youth Ministries. He is one of the founding organizers of See You at the Pole, involving 3,000,000 students each year in prayer. Under his leadership, the National Network of Youth Ministries coordinates Challenge 2000, an evangelism project uniting youth ministries to cooperate in spreading the good news of the gospel to every teenager in every school nationwide by the end of the year 2000. Paul and his wife, Toni, live in San Diego, California, with their two sons.

Siv Ricketts, author of the student article, "How to Leave a Mark on Your School," is a student ministries director, freelance writer and editor living in San Diego, California. Siv and her husband, Dave, have been ministering to students together for the past six years and have recently been blessed with a new son, Corban.

Natalie Chenault, author of the student devotionals, enjoys diet soda and pudding cups. She attends Eastern College and loves hanging out with junior highers. She hopes to appear on *Jeopardy!* one day.

....You've Made the Right Choice in Choosing Pulse for Your Junior Highers

The Top Ten Reasons...

10. Junior highers equate who God is with what church is like. To them a boring youth ministry means a boring God.

    Fun and variety are the twin threads that weave their way through this curriculum's every page.

9. Junior highers need and deserve youth workers who are expert trainers and teachers of biblical truth.

    Every book is pulsating with youth leader tips and a full-length youth worker article designed to infuse YOU with more passion and skill for your ministry to junior highers.

8. Junior highers need ongoing reminders of the big idea of each session.

    Wouldn't it be great if you could give your students devotionals every week to reinforce the learning goals of the session? Get this: YOU CAN because THIS CURRICULUM DOES.

7. Some of our world's most effective evangelists are junior highers.

    Every session, and we mean EVERY session, concludes with an evangelism option that ties "the big idea" of the session to the big need to share Christ with others.

1. Junior highers are moving through all sorts of changes—from getting a new body to getting a new locker.

   We've designed a curriculum that revolves around one simple vision: moving God's Word into a junior high world.

2. Junior highers tend to understand the Bible in bits and pieces and miss the big picture of all that God has done for them.

   This curriculum follows a strategic three-year plan that walks junior highers through the Bible, stopping at the most important points along the way.

3. Tragically, most junior highers are under challenged in their walks with Christ.

   We've packed the final step of each session with three options that serve to move students a few steps forward in their walks with Christ.

4. Junior highers learn best when they can see, taste, feel and experience the session.

   This curriculum involves students in every step through active learning and games to prove to students that following Christ is the greatest adventure ever.

5. Junior highers' growing minds are ready for more than just fun and games with a little Scripture thrown in.

   Scripture is the very skeleton of each session, giving it its shape, its form and its very life.

6. Since no two junior highers (or their leaders) look, think or act alike, no two junior high ministries look, think or act alike.

   Each step comes with three options that you can cut and paste to create a session that works best for YOUR students and YOUR personality.

Moving Through Pulse

Since **Pulse** is vibrating with so many different learning activities, this guide will help you pick and choose the best possible options for *your* students.

The Sessions

The six sessions are split into two stand-alone units, so you can choose to teach either three or six sessions at a time. Each session is geared to be 45 to 90 minutes long and is comprised of the following four steps.

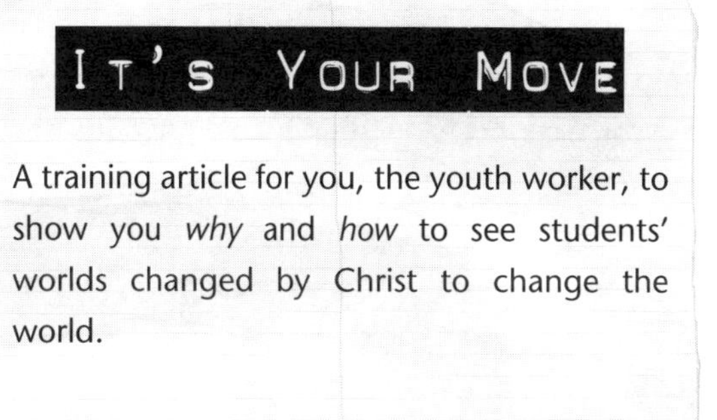

It's Your Move

A training article for you, the youth worker, to show you *why* and *how* to see students' worlds changed by Christ to change the world.

This first step helps students focus in on the theme of the lesson in a fun and engaging way through three options:

Move It—An active learning experience that may or may not involve all of your students.

Chat Room—Provocative, clear and simple questions to get your students thinking and chatting.

Fun and Games—Zany, creative and competitive games that may or may not involve all of your students.

The second step enables students to look up to God by relating the very words of Scripture to the session topic through three options:

Move It—An active learning experience that may or may not involve all of your students.

Chat Room—Provocative, clear and simple questions to get your students chatting about the Scripture lesson.

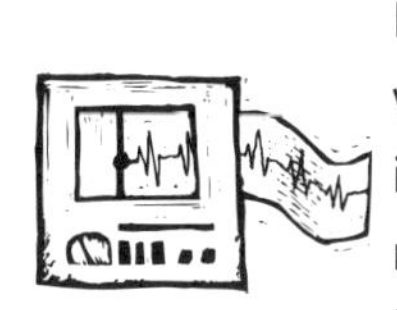

Pulse Points—A message outline with simple points and meaningful illustrations to give students some massive truths about Scripture with hardly any preparation on your part.

This step asks students to look inward and discover how God's Word connects with their own worlds through three options:

Chat Room—Provocative, clear and simple questions to get your students chatting.

Real Life—A case study about someone (usually a junior higher) who needs your students' help figuring out what to do.

Tough Questions—Four to six mind-stretching questions that challenge students to a new level of depth and integration.

This final step leads students out into their world with specific challenges to apply at school, at home and with their friends through three options based on your students' growth potential:

Light the Fire—For junior highers who may or may not be Christians and need easily accessible application ideas.

Fired Up—For students who are definitely Christians and are ready for more intense application ideas.

Spread the Fire—A special evangelism application idea for students with a passion to see others come to know Christ.

Other Important Moving Parts

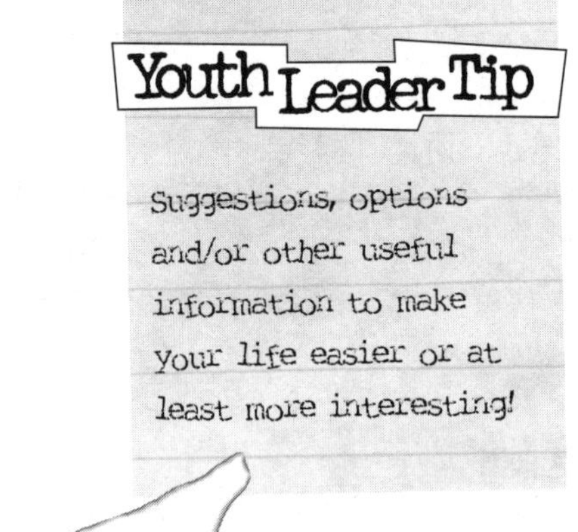

Devotions in Motion

Week Five: Grace

Four devotionals for each session to keep the big idea moving through your junior highers' lives all week long.

On the Move—An appealing, easy-to-read handout you can give your junior highers to help them learn how to leave a mark on their schools by being salt and light for classmates and faculty.

LEADER'S ARTICLE LEADER'S ARTICLE LEADER'S ARTICLE

Helping Students Make a Difference on Campus

It was back in the days of town criers and telephone switchboards. Every day at about the same time the operator of the switchboard received a call from a man who asked her the time of day.

One day she inquired, "I'm curious. I don't mind giving you the time, but why do you ask me every day?" "Oh, that's simple," he answered, "You see, it is my job to ring the town bell, and I just want to be sure I ring it on time!" "How ironic," replied the operator, "because I set my watch by your bell!"

What a picture of most of today's society—and especially of teenagers! You know the tremendous influence teenagers have upon one another. But the sad thing is that unless we challenge them to think differently, they could be swept down the path of least resistance. It's way too easy to just go with the flow.

We want to invite students today to make a difference in their world—to become thermostats in a world of thermometers! A thermometer merely measures the temperature around it. But a thermostat *influences* the temperature. Something has been programmed into it internally according to a master plan. Our master plan is the Great Commission—a high calling to cooperate with the Almighty God to be His ambassadors on earth (see Matthew 28:18-20; 2 Corinthians 5:20). We must find ways to internalize a desire to fulfill that high calling within our young people.

Why? Because they are the key to reaching the most responsive mission field on earth. George Barna reports that 6 out of 10 teenagers want to be close to God and that 75 percent who receive Christ do so by age 17. Yet only one-third of them are involved in a Christian youth group. That means that if the Great Commission is to be fulfilled we must reach young people. And the best way to reach them is by helping teenagers reach their friends where they spend most of their time—at school.

There are many things you can do to help program the thermostat in the heart of your teenagers. You know the basics: prayer, the Word of God, training and discipleship. But let me emphasize two other priorities that are particularly important in my experience.

Big Picture

Give your students the gift of vision. They probably won't understand the priority of the Great Commission unless you explain it from your heart. It is more than inviting friends to a concert; it is a message backed up by a life. Somehow we must instill in them the sense of urgency, the need to cooperate with God, and the crucial role they play as missionaries to their schools.

When I was a high school sophomore, my youth leader told a group of us, "If you don't reach your campus for Christ, no one else will!" As I went home, those words would not go away. Before I could sleep that night, I fell to my knees praying for our group, my friends and the many who weren't Christians at my school. I began to weep. I really wanted my friends to know Christ. To this day, that burden has never left me—all because my youth leader helped me own the vision of what God wanted to do on my campus.

Believe in Them

Give your students the gift of affirmation. Most adolescents are very insecure. That's why a big part of the impact we have will come from simply communicating how much we care for and have confidence in them.

God has a special love and purpose for young people. He always has—consider David, Daniel, Esther and Mary, to name a few. There is reason to believe in them! One modern-day teenager from Georgia named Emily prayed "Dear Jesus, I commit to give my whole year to changing my school for You." That simple prayer, echoed by two others, was enough to motivate the three of them to start a club called C.A.M.P.U.S.—Christians Actively Mobilizing to Penetrate Unreached Students. They met weekly that year for prayer, accountability, encouragement and discipleship. And the results? Emily shares:

> *I can't begin to tell how awesomely God moved in my school. We saw person after person get saved. We each picked one unsaved friend and targeted them until they personally got to know Jesus as their Savior. Last year we saw Jesus' love spread through the hallways and into the classrooms. It's working. I'm not changing my high school. My friends aren't changing my high school. God is changing my high school. Through Him all things are possible!*

When we invest in our students, they really will make a difference!

—Paul Fleischmann

SESSIONONESESSIONONESESSIONONESESSIONONE

The Big Idea

Prayer can help you deal with any type of stress at school.

Session Aims

In this session you will guide students to:

- Learn what causes stress and how to respond to it;
- Feel stress (just kidding!)—feel encouraged that their stress levels can be lowered;
- Identify stressful areas in their daily lives and make plans to move past the stress.

"Do not be anxious about anything, but in everything, by prayer and petition, with thanksgiving, present your requests to God. And the peace of God, which transcends all understanding, will guard your hearts and your minds in Christ Jesus." Philippians 4:6,7

Other Important Verses

Genesis 22:1-14; Exodus 1:22—2:4; Ruth 1; 1 Samuel 1:1-17; 2 Kings 22:1—23:3; Job 1:1-3,13-22; Philippians 4:4-7

STEP MOVING IN

This step gets students thinking about the stress they experience at school.

Option 1 Move It

You'll need A smile on your face and a song in your heart!

Greet students and explain that you're going to read a list of things that might cause stress at school. Have them stand and respond to each item in one of three ways: Put their hands on their hips and say, "No stress"; wave one hand in the air and say, "Some stress"; or wave both hands in the air and shout, "Major stress!"

Be sure that everyone participates after each item as you quickly read the following list:

- **Getting ready for school in the morning**
- **Gym class**
- **Talking to someone you like at lunch**
- **Surprise quizzes**
- **Spilling your drink on your lap at lunch**
- **Science class**
- **Finding a book in the library**
- **Being paired with a really popular kid for your science project**
- **Essay exams**
- **Mystery meat in the cafeteria**
- **Finding out you've had a booger hanging from your nose for the past half hour**
- **English class**
- **History class**
- **Forgetting your locker combination**
- **Word problems in math**
- **Getting all your homework done**
- **Lunch period**
- **Being called to the principal's office**
- **Tripping in the hallway and dropping all your books**
- **Five-page book reports**
- **Tripping at lunch and dropping all your food**
- **Giving an oral report**

Invite students to suggest other possible stress triggers and as each one is called out, have everyone respond as before. Transition to the next step by explaining: **We all go through stress, but having a relationship with Jesus can help you react to stress differently. Your stress level can stay lower when you turn stressful situations over to God in prayer, especially in the place where you spend most of your waking hours right now—school.**

Option 2 Chat Room

You'll need Copies of "School Stress Scorecard" (p. 21) and pens or pencils.

Greet students and explain that you're starting a new series on life at school. Distribute "School Stress Scorecard" and pens or pencils; then allow three to five minutes for students to complete the handout. Discuss students' answers; then ask several to share which stress maker is number one on their lists. Discuss the top choices and why they are stress producing for some students.

Note: Be sensitive to students who may find some things stressful that other students may not. For instance, one student might find running a mile during gym class to be extremely stressful; another might relish the chance to show off—both in gym class and in your youth group!

Explain: **Different things create stress for different people. For example, Dan might not be stressed by an essay exam; Tom might not be stressed by pairing up for square dancing. No matter what your specific stress triggers are, today we're going to discover how to overcome them.**

Option 3 Fun and Games

You'll need Six chairs and one copy of "School Stress Melodrama" (p. 22).

Ahead of time, place six chairs in a traditional classroom setup, angled sideways at the front of the room so the audience can see the performance.

Greet students and recruit seven to nine volunteers to act out the following roles as you read an impromptu melodrama: Jim, a normal kid dealing with a very stressful day; Jim's mind, hovering around Jim making suggestions; two to four of Jim's friends; Mrs. Cranfield, Jim's math teacher; Mr. Pritchit, the assistant school principal; and Jenny, a really popular girl. **Note:** Instruct actors to repeat any spoken lines for their parts after you read them and to act out their parts with enthusiasm!

After the melodrama, wait for the roaring applause to subside; then invite the whole group to share what types of issues create stress for junior highers. Some answers might include: tests, grades, peer acceptance, parental expectations, etc. Transition to the next step by explaining: **No matter what your specific stress triggers are, today we're going to discover how to overcome them.**

Youth Leader Tip

In a 1998 survey of 600 teens, one of the three greatest challenges 13- to 14-year-olds identified was—you guessed it!—stress. The other two were friendship and school. (Statistics from a privately commissioned report, *Teenagers Describe Their Church Youth Group: A Study of U.S. Teens, Ages 13 to 18* [Ventura, CA: The Barna Research Group, Ltd., Fall 1998], p. 9.)

This step shows that the best response to stress is prayer, remembering God is in control.

You'll need Several Bibles and, of course, this irreplaceable resource we call **Pulse**!

Divide students into groups of 5 to 10 and distribute a Bible to anyone who didn't bring one. Have everyone follow along closely as you read Job 1:1-3,13-22. After you've finished reading, instruct each group to put together a 30-second TV commercial presenting a solution for stress based on the story of Job. **Note:** Hint that the primary solution to stress—both in action and attitude— is found in verse 21 (the action is prayer and the attitude is that God is in control). Circulate around the room, making sure the groups understand what they're supposed to be doing and see that they're staying on track.

Allow five to seven minutes of preparation; then have the groups present their commercials one at a time. Make sure you (and the rest of the students) give them lots of support and applause for their efforts! Once the commercials have all been presented, discuss:

What do we learn about Job in Job 1? He was a great man who feared God; he was very obedient to God.

Youth Leader Tip

Make sure students know what stress is! Here's a simple definition: a demand that is placed upon someone that causes him or her to feel anxious or nervous.

What trials caused stress for Job? Just a few things! He lost everything: his possessions, his workers and all his children.

Why would losing all of that cause stress? Times of pain and loss are very stressful, as are surprises.

What was the first thing Job did when he heard the dis-STRESS-ing news? His first reaction was to worship God.

Did Job try to change the situation right away? No.

Did Job grumble or complain? No.

Did Job get angry? No, again!

Did Job pretend it was no big deal? No way—he tore his robes and shaved his head, the ultimate signs of sorrow in his culture.

What action did Job take? He prayed and worshiped God.

What attitude did Job have? He realized that God knew what He was doing.

How would you explain Job's words in verse 21 to a six-year-old? (Expect a variety of explanations here and affirm students' answers.)

Option 2 Chat Room

You'll need Several Bibles.

Distribute Bibles and invite students to follow along as you read Job 1:1-3,13-22; then discuss:

What do we learn about Job in Job 1? He was a great man who feared God; he was very obedient to God.

What trials caused stress for Job? Just a few things! He lost everything: his possessions, his workers and all his children.

Why would losing all of that cause stress? Times of pain and loss are very stressful, as are surprises.

What was the first thing Job did when he heard the dis-STRESS-ing news? His first reaction was to worship God.

Did Job try to change the situation right away? No.

Did Job grumble or complain? No.

Did Job get angry? No, again!

Did Job pretend it was no big deal? No way—he tore his robes and shaved his head, the ultimate signs of sorrow in his culture.

What action did Job take? He prayed and worshiped God.

What attitude did Job have? He realized that God knew what He was doing.

How would you explain Job's words in verse 21 to a six-year-old? (Expect a variety of explanations here and affirm students' answers.)

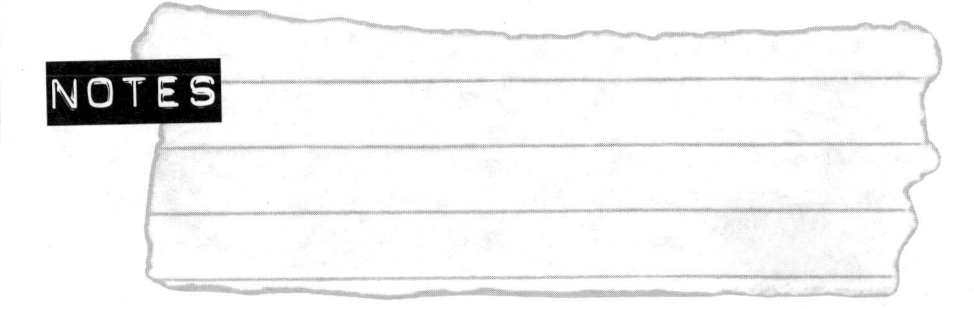

Youth Leader Tip

Team Ministry! This might seem like a "no duh, totally obvious" teaching tip, but it's amazing how often I can forget the obvious (are you anything like me?). Ministry—and teachin—to young teens is always more effective when you have a *team* of adult leaders. This is crucial to relational ministry. You'll also find it makes small-group exercises, like this Job commercial on stress, 732 percent more effective (guaranteed!) when you have an adult or mature high school student in each group to help guide the process. The leader shouldn't do the work for the kids; the role of the leader is to *facilitate*. You often don't need a person in this role when dealing with older teens, but it sure helps with junior highers!

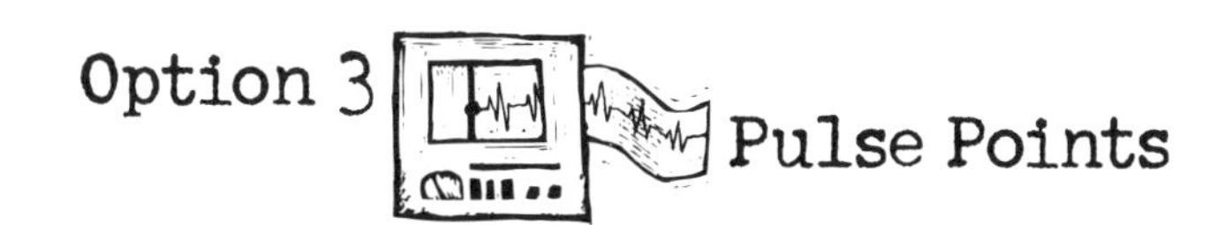

You'll need Several Bibles (go figure that you might need *those* for a Bible-based curriculum!).

The Big Idea

We are all faced with demands that make us feel stress, but there's a way to reduce it or get rid of it altogether.

The Big Question

What is the right reaction when we feel stress?

Explain to students that knowing how to handle stress at school is all about body language. Ask if anyone knows what body language is. After the giggling subsides, explain that it's expressing feelings through the way you position your body and facial expressions. Explain: **Body language communicates a ton of unspoken feelings—often more than our words themselves could communicate.** To illustrate this, strike a few different poses and have students guess what you're communicating. You should be able to communicate the following emotions and attitudes: boredom, impatience, anger, fear, joy and superiority. Afterward, get down on your knees (yes, really) and share the following:

> **Note:** There's actually scientific evidence to prove that young teens are really bad at detecting emotion from body language—though they don't realize it. Don't be concerned about whether or not students identify the emotions you're trying to convey. It's more important that they understand the *concept* that posture communicates.

1. During stressful times, the right *action* is worship and prayer.

Explain: **God wants us to bring our problems and our stress to Him. Sometimes He'll just take our problems and stress away from us and sometimes He won't—but even when He doesn't, He is always right there with us in the midst of our stress.**

Distribute Bibles and continue: **We don't have to be on our knees to pray for God to be with us during stressful times. Prayer is an awesome thing—we can do it anywhere at any time!** Ask for a volunteer to read Philippians 4:4-7; then point out that Paul isn't just making a suggestion in this passage—the two verbs ("do" and "present") that he uses are actually *commands*. Transition to the next point by explaining that the action step for prayer is part of the proper body position for stress relief and that we also need to have the right attitude.

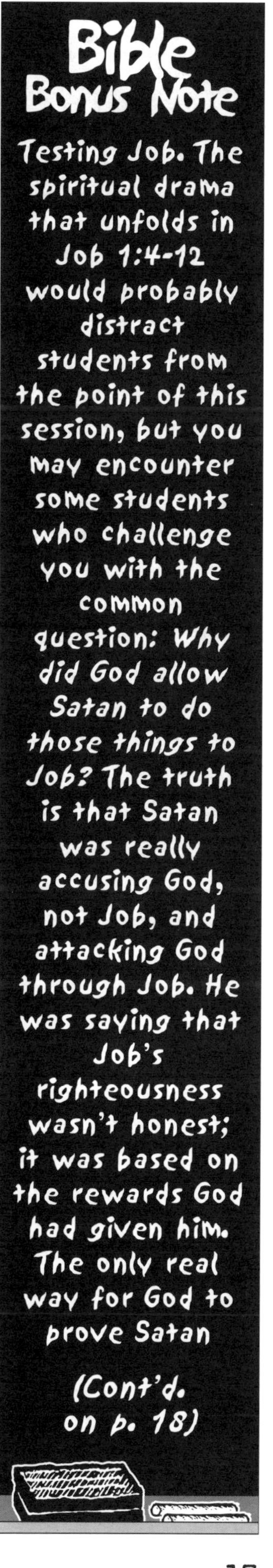

Bible Bonus Note

(Cont'd. from p. 17)

false is through Job. The main purpose of Job's suffering was to become an example of God's power and might—and even though this may not have been completely clear to Job at the time, he accepted that God was ultimately in control.

2. During stressful times, the right *attitude* is *God is in control.*

Explain: **When we have the attitude of trusting God that He is in total control over our lives, we're showing respect for Him. When the Bible talks about respecting God, it's referring to the posture of actually lying facedown on the ground in from of Him.**

Demonstrate lying facedown in front of God while you explain that it's the *attitude* of the body position that is important, not the position itself. Explain: **When you lie facedown in front of someone, you are defenseless—you are communicating that you have complete trust in the person in front of you. God wants us to have this kind of trust in Him all the time. He doesn't require that you lie facedown in the middle of a stressful math test—all He asks is that you surrender to Him in your heart and mind.**

Return to Philippians 4 and point out that this attitude of trust is obvious in Paul's words. When we are told to bring our needs to God, we can trust Him to help us.

> **Note:** Refer to this step's options 1 and 2 for expansion on action and attitude through Job's story.

This step helps students consider their own reactions to stress.

You'll need A white board, a dry-erase marker, paper and pens or pencils.

Divide students into groups of three to five and distribute the paper and pens or pencils. Ask students to write down as many things as they can think of that create stress for young teens at school. Allow three to five minutes; then invite groups to share their lists and write down their ideas on the white board. One at a time, invite discussions about how junior highers can combat stress in each particular situation and remind students that the *action* of worship and prayer and the *attitude* that God is in control are the first two steps to combat stress.

Explain: **There are often practical steps we can take to combat stress, too—especially if the stress is a result of our own poor choices. For instance, if a history test is stressing you out, *first* you need to pray and trust God; then you need to study hard, get enough sleep the night before and eat healthy food on the day of the test. You can also study with a partner and ask your teacher for extra help with anything you don't understand. If you think about it, there's always something practical you can do to reduce your stress—even if it doesn't disappear completely.**

You'll need Just this here book—yes, indeedy, it's a keeper!

Share the following case study:

> **Brad is a big ball of stress. The guy just can't seem to shake it! His stress cycle is always the same: At night he stresses about getting his homework done and deciding what he'll wear the next day that will be acceptable to other kids; and at school he's concerned about getting good grades, about being accepted by his teachers and classmates and about not saying anything stupid. To top it all off, Brad stresses about being short! His youth leader told him to pray about his stress, but that doesn't seem like much of a solution to Brad.**

Discuss:

What's the main cause of Brad's stress? He's insecure and worries about meeting the expectations and standards of others.

Can Brad ever be totally free of stress? The truth is that life is full of things that can stress us out—that's what makes it challenging! The key is to alleviate the things that *we* do that add to our stress levels.

What things could Brad do to alleviate his stress? It's hard to break the habit of worrying about what everyone else thinks, but there are things that Brad can do right away: He can pray about the things he worries about; he can set aside enough time to get his homework done (which may include not watching his favorite half-hour sitcom at 9 P.M.); and he can show respect to his teachers and earn their respect by simply doing his best in their classes.

You'll need An uncluttered mind!

Ahead of time, lather, rinse, repeat!

1. **What if I pray about my stress and nothing changes?** The answer to this question goes back to a theology of prayer: God *always* answers our prayers; His response is either yes, no or wait. That's where the whole trust issue comes in. We must trust that if God doesn't remove the cause of our stress, He must have a purpose for it in our lives—*or* it could be the result of our own continued bad choices!

2. **Is stress my fault or someone else's?** Of course, stress can come from either, but it's usually a combination of both. For example, a pop quiz can be pretty stressful—and even more so if you haven't been paying attention in class and doing your homework!

3. **Is it really possible to be totally stress free?** Um, no! At least not on *this* planet. It's important to understand that just when we get rid of stress in one area of our lives, it crops up somewhere else. It's usually cyclical—it comes and goes. Jesus helps us to get through these cycles without losing our minds!

This step gives students the chance to choose better ways to respond to their stress this week.

You'll need Copies of "My Stress Prayer" (p. 24) and pens or pencils.

Divide students into groups of three to five and distribute "My Stress Prayer" and pens or pencils. Instruct students to write down one area of stress in their lives at school; then allow five minutes for students to share their stress areas within their groups and have groups discuss action steps for each member's stress area.

Close with a group prayer, beginning with your own petition about a stress area in your life; then extend an invitation for students who are willing to share what they've written on their handouts to pray.

You'll need Several Bibles, a white board, a dry-erase marker, paper and pens or pencils.

Ahead of time, write the following Bible characters and their Scripture references on the white board: Abraham (Genesis 22:1-14); Moses' mom (Exodus 1:22—2:4); Ruth (Ruth 1); Hannah (1 Samuel 1:1-17); and Josiah (2 Kings 22:1—23:3).

Are your students ready for a little extra challenge? Here it is! Divide students into groups of three to five and distribute Bibles, paper and pens or pencils. Point out what you've written on the white board and explain that the Bible has some real-life case studies of stressful challenges and situations. Instruct students to look up the passages and write out the stressors in each of the characters' lives, how the characters handled the stress and whether or not each character handled the stress well. Allow a few minutes for research; then briefly discuss each group's findings.

Close by instructing students to share one thing with their groups that they can do differently when they feel stressed out this week and then to pray for each person in their groups.

You'll need Some enthusiastic students who want their friends to know Jesus!

To be completely honest, this session has been somewhat self-centered. It has focused exclusively on students' individual stress levels. Let's turn the tables now and focus on outreach!

Begin by leading a discussion focusing on the stress in the lives of other people and how students can help alleviate that stress. Explain: **As hard as it might be to admit, often we *add* stress to people's lives! As agents of our Lord, Jesus Christ, we can bring peace, calm, comfort, support and encouragement instead.**

Ask students to think of one non-Christian friend or relative who is experiencing stress in some area of his or her life and to consider ways that they can help alleviate that stress. Remind students that the *first* actions must be praying and turning the stress over to God.

Close in prayer, asking God to enable students to identify stress in other people's lives and to have the courage to share the good news that Jesus is where to turn when we need help with our stress!

School Stress Scorecard

Rank the following possible stress creators in order from 1 (most stressful) to 15 (least stressful).

- [ ] Your teacher announces a pop quiz—and you haven't done your homework for two days.
- [ ] Everyone in gym class has to run the mile today—timed.
- [ ] You've been daydreaming in English—and your teacher calls on you to answer a question you didn't hear.
- [ ] You've been asked to cheat on a test—by the most popular kid in school.
- [ ] You need to get into your locker in between classes—and you've forgotten the combination.
- [ ] You have a book report due tomorrow—and you haven't even started reading the book.
- [ ] The principal's voice comes over the PA system—and calls you to the office.
- [ ] You're struggling to bring your grade up in a class—and the test tomorrow is worth one fourth of your final grade.
- [ ] Your teacher just handed you a huge test—and it's all essay questions.
- [ ] The toughest kid in school shoved you into your locker this morning—and told you to meet him (or her!) in the parking lot after school.
- [ ] There's a big party this weekend and all your friends are going—but you weren't invited.
- [ ] You've got a zit the size of Mt. Everest—right on the end of your nose.
- [ ] Time to learn square dancing in gym class—with partners of the opposite gender.
- [ ] Report cards come out today.
- [ ] One of your teachers has a major problem with you—but you have no idea why.

School Stress Melodrama

It's another day at Pesky Middle School and Jim and his friends are teasing each other and joking around while making their way into third-period math class. Just before sitting down, Jim trips on his own feet and falls flat on the floor—and all of his friends point at him and laugh like crazy!

Mrs. Cranfield, the math teacher, gets mad and snaps, "Jim, stop that goofing around and sit down *right this minute!*"

Jim stands up, straightens out his clothes and sits down as quickly as he can—which turns out to be a bit too quickly and his chair falls over.

Mrs. Cranfield is pretty irritated by now and is convinced Jim is goofing off. She yells, "Jim, if you don't stop this nonsense, I'm going to call Mr. Pritchit!"

Jim's mind yells, *C'mon you idiot! Just sit down and stop being such a klutz.*

Finally, Jim sits down and just as he begins to relax, Jenny, a really popular girl, walks up and says, "Um, I think you're in my seat."

Jim is totally embarrassed and rushes to get out of the girl's seat. He jumps up and bumps right into Jenny, knocking all of her books out of her arms. Jenny begins to cry—loudly. All of Jim's friends start laughing again.

Loser, loser, loser, Jim's mind is whispering. Mrs. Cranfield is stomping her foot on the floor and shouting, "That's enough, that's enough, that's *enough!*"

Jim locates another seat; Jenny finally stops crying; Jim's friends stop laughing; and everything seems OK—until Mrs. Cranfield announces, "I've got a surprise for you today: a pop quiz!"

Everyone groans and Jim's mind says, *Hey, bonehead, why didn't you study last night instead of watching the* Star Trek *marathon on TV?* Jim groans even louder than the rest of the class.

As Mrs. Cranfield passes out the quiz, she insists on complete silence. Jim suddenly realizes that he has to use the restroom—immediately! He raises his hand and Mrs. Cranfield impatiently asks, "What *now*, Jim?"

"May I be excused to the restroom?" Jim answers.

Jim's friends snicker. His mind taunts, *Yeah, like she's gonna let you go anywhere!*

"Absolutely not!" Mrs. Cranfield replies. "You sit right where you are and finish that quiz. You may leave when you are finished."

Jenny shakes her head and gives Jim a "what planet are you from?" look while Jim nervously squirms in his seat to keep from bursting until he finishes the quiz.

"Hey, Jimbo, what's the answer to number six?" Jim's friend whispers while Jim's mind is chanting, *Restroom, restroom, gotta go, gotta go,* over and over.

"Jimbo! Hey, Jimbo!" he hears from across the aisle.

Gotta go, gotta go!

"What's the answer? C'mon, help me out!"

Jenny's giving him that look again.

Restroom, restroom, gotta go, gotta go.

"Jimbo, help me out here!"

"Stop it!" shouts Jim. "I don't *know* the answer to number six!"

Everyone stops and stares at Jim. Mrs. Cranfield picks up the phone and summons Mr. Pritchit to the classroom.

When he arrives, Mr. Pritchit stands at the front of the room and he and Mrs. Cranfield whisper while Jim's mind asks, *What were you thinking, you big dork?*

Jim's friends are looking at him like he's the biggest jerk in the world, and Jenny is shaking her head as Jim tries to disappear by sinking as low as he can into his seat.

Finally, Mr. Pritchit walks over to Jim and says, "Let's go, Jim. It looks like you've really done it this time."

Jim stands up too quickly and he bumps Mr. Pritchit, knocking him into two other students.

Jim's mind says, *Boy, oh boy, you should have stayed in bed this morning!*

My Stress Prayer

One area of my life where I'm experiencing stress at school right now is:

Here are some things I can do that might reduce this stress:

1.

2.

3.

4.

5.

In the space below, write a prayer to God and ask Him to help you with this stress:

Dear God,

Amen.

FasT FacTs

Spring on over To Luke 12:22-31.

God Says

Hali was The biggesT whaT if person in The whole school. She was always worried abouT someThing. WhaT if The Teacher gave us a pop quiz in MaTh? WhaT if They ran ouT of food aT lunch? WhaT if The guy she liked didn'T like her back? WhaT if her school ran ouT of yearbooks before she had a chance To geT one? And on and on and on.

I Do

The whaT if quesTions of life will geT To you if you leT Them. IT's a good Thing Jesus gives us some preTTy sTrong words abouT worrying abouT The fuTure. InsTead of Thinking abouT whaT mighT go wrong, He inviTes us To Think abouT His kingdom and TrusT Him To Take care of Things.

Today when you sTarT To worry abouT someThing, Think abouT Jesus as quickly as you can. JusT ThaT quickly you can release your worries To Him and be comforTed! Amazing, huh?

FOLD HERE

Devotions in Motion

WEEK ONE: STRESSED - OUT!

Quick QuesTions

Flip open your Bible abouT To iTs middle and read Psalm 37:8,9.

God Says

WhaT's The biggesT problem wiTh sTress?

A. IT mighT give you a sTomachache and a headache.
B. IT keeps you awake aT nighT when you should be having sweeT dreams.
C. IT keeps you from relying and TrusTing on God.
D. IT makes you hungry so you snack on The Three Cs: chips, candy and cookies.

I Do

AlThough (A), (B), and (D) mighT be problems, iT's really (C) ThaT is The biggesT problem wiTh sTress. As The PsalmisT warns, freT-Ting leads To all sorTs of wrong. IT's ulTimaTely a message ThaT you don'T TrusT God and believe He's in conTrol.

WhaT is worrying you The mosT Today? Spend a few minuTes praying, Thanking God for His goodness, and asking His will To be done in whaTever you're worried abouT.

DAY 2

Fast Facts

If you're hungry, flip To John 6:1-15.

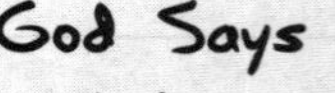

God Says

You don't know what you're going to do. You've got a slumber party tomorrow night and everything is going wrong. A few people are sick and might not be able to come; your mom bought all the wrong food; and to top it all off, your little sister, who was supposed to be gone on a church overnighter, has decided that she'd rather stay home and hang out with you—and your mom's letting her! Ugh. You can feel your heart start to pound and your stomach start to tense up. What do you do?

I Do

How about trusting God? He'll take care of all of your needs, just like He did when the people were hungry in John 6:1-15. He might take care of them differently than you expect; after all, no one thought that those few loaves and fish would feed all those people. And yet God did it!

What is causing you stress today? Ask God to remind you whenever you feel stress that He's going to take care of you. He might just surprise you in the creative and cool ways that He does it, too!

Quick Questions

Oh my goodness! You won't believe what happens in Daniel 3:1-30.

God Says

What's the toughest situation you might face today at school?

- ❑ Spilling a drink in your lap, leaving a really embarrassing wet stain
- ❑ The friend that you've had since fourth grade making fun of the Christian T-shirt you're wearing
- ❑ Your locker mate making fun of the pictures you have hanging in your locker right in front of someone you have a crush on
- ❑ Being thrown into a fire and left to die

I Do

Well, none of those situations would be fun, but you'll probably agree that the last one would be the worst. And yet that actually happened to Shadrach, Mesach and Abednego as you can read for yourself in Daniel 3:16-23. Those young men had such trust in God that they knew He could save them; but even if He didn't, they would still trust Him. That's a pretty good way to get rid of stress.

Spend time praying today about something that's stressing you out, remembering that if God can save three buddies from a fire, He can handle whatever you're going through, too.

FOLD HERE

SessionTwoSessionTwoSessionTwoSessionTwo

The Big Idea

Living by the Spirit makes you different from others at your school.

Session Aims

In this session you will guide students to:

- Learn that Christians *should* be different from nonbelievers;
- Wrestle with their feelings about fitting in and being different;
- Choose some alien implications they're willing to try out this week.

Alien Invasion!

The Biggest Verse

"And they admitted that they were aliens and strangers on earth." Hebrews 11:13

Other Important Verses

Galatians 5:16-26; Hebrews 11:13-16; 1 Peter 2:11,12

This step introduces the concept of being different.

You'll need A white board and a dry-erase marker (or another way to list the five "customs" so students can remember them).

Greet students and divide them into an even number of groups with no less than three, but no more than 12 students in each group. Explain that each group is an alien culture from a different planet and needs to come up with five "customs" from its planet; then write the following list on the white board:

1. A handshake or some other way to greet other people
2. A new word of greeting instead of "hello" or "hi"
3. Three things that really offend you (something that other people do all the time and would be likely to do during the first 30 seconds of talking to them)
4. The acceptable way to sit
5. How to respond when someone asks a question

Allow three to five minutes for groups to figure out their customs; then instruct specific groups to visit with other groups (Group One visits Group Two, etc.). Groups will visit for three minutes; then switch. Do this two or three times, depending on the number of groups and the amount time you have.

When they're finished, have everyone return to their seats and discuss:

Which was the strangest group?

Which group was the most normal?

Have you ever been in another country and found the rules of behavior different from what you are used to? If anyone has, invite him or her to describe what was different.

Transition to the next step by explaining: **Although we're probably not as strange as some of these groups were, some of the choices we make at school might be different from our friends.**

You'll need A bed sheet, a table, several blindfolds, paper plates and several food items from different ethnic cultures (such as burritos, egg rolls, pizza, sushi, gyro sandwiches, chicken curry and anything else you can come up with).

Ahead of time, cut the food items into bite-sized pieces and place one piece of each kind of food on each paper plate so that you will have five plates with the same varieties of food on them. Place the plates on the table and cover the food with the sheet to hide it.

Welcome students and ask if anyone is hungry (good luck finding anyone who isn't!). Invite five volunteers to come forward and have them stand behind the table facing the rest of the group. Blindfold the volunteers and uncover the plates of food. Place a plate in front of each volunteer and when you give the signal, have them start tasting the food on the plates and naming the country or ethnic group the food is from. After each food item's origin has successfully been identified, have volunteers remove their blindfolds and return to their seats. Explain: **There are lots of other things besides food that make ethnic cultures different from one another.** Discuss:

Have any of you ever been to another country?

Have any of you experienced or heard of ways of behaving that are different in other countries than in ours?

Why do you think different countries and cultures develop such different ideas about acceptable behavior?

What would you do if you went to another country and found out that you were offending people by the way you acted?

Explain: **Today we're going to look at ways that being a Christian might make us seem different from everybody else around us. Although we don't want to offend people, we do want to do what God tells us to do, even if it means sticking out from those around us.**

Option 3 Fun and Games

You'll need A candy or food prize for the winning team (optional).

There are a couple of ways you can play this game, depending on the size of the group. If there are fewer than six students, you can play this as one of those stand-up-and-move-around games ("go to the left wall if you think the answer is fake; go to the right wall if you think the answer is real"). If you have a medium-sized group (6 to 15 students), play with two teams. If your group is larger, this is a great game to play with multiple small teams competing against each other. Regardless of the way you choose to play, teams will need to decide whether the statements are fake or real.

The following items are statements about behavior in other countries. Read them one at a time, and have students or teams respond whether they think the statements are real or fake. Award 100 points for each correct answer.

> **Note to youth leaders outside the United States:** If your country is listed below, substitute your country's statement with the following: **People in the United States tend to be loud, rude and obnoxious.** Real!

- **In Argentina, it's polite to greet people, even people you don't know, by kissing them on the cheek.** Real.
- **In Iceland, it's not considered rude to sneeze on someone.** Fake.
- **People from the South Pacific island of Tangano pinch each other's cheeks to say hello.** Fake, there's no such island!
- **In Ireland, saying, "Let's have some crack" means, "Let's have a fun time."** Real, but it's spelled differently.
- **In some Middle Eastern countries, you can compliment the cook by belching after a big meal.** Real.
- **When people from Greenland say, "Your hair is showing," it really means, "Stop making a fool of yourself."** Fake.
- **In England, people hold their fork in their left hand and their knife in their right hand while eating. They never hold their fork with their right hand.** Real.
- **In the Bahamas, it's not appropriate to go to the beach on Sunday.** Real.
- **Tiberian women never speak in public.** Fake.
- **In Zimbabwe, it's considered impolite to smile at someone you don't know.** Fake.
- **In Denmark and Holland, french fries are served with mayonnaise, not ketchup.** Real.
- **Russian men greet each other with a big ol' kiss on the lips.** Real.
- **In most countries other than the United States, you'd never ask to use the restroom or bathroom; you'd ask for the toilet.** Real.

Award the prizes to the team with the most points; then transition to the next step by explaining: **Each day junior highers enter a place where they make a zillion choices about how they are going to act—it's the world of school.**

Youth Leader Tip

Blend in or stick out? This lesson is built around the scriptural idea that as citizens of heaven, our behavior should be different. Some students will be drawn to this simply because they love to be original, noticed and unique, rather than understanding the concept itself. Others (usually the majority of them) would rather blend in with the crowd—and the idea of being different will seem foreign (no pun intended) and uncomfortable to them, so they will shy away from it. Be aware of these two types of students and make sure to communicate that the point of the lesson is to not just be unique for the sake of being unique!

This step helps students understand that as Christians, we're strangers on earth.

You'll need Several Bibles, copies of "Alien Questionnaire" (p. 36), pens or pencils and two to six sharp adult volunteers who are very familiar with the characters from Hebrews 11.

> **Note:** OK, we admit it—this option requires more preparation, and you can't decide to do it on the spur of the moment; but it's worth the effort!

Ahead of time, assign adult volunteers the roles of some of the Old Testament saints mentioned in Hebrews 11 (there are 16 saints mentioned specifically by name: Abel, Enoch, Noah, Abraham, Isaac, Jacob, Esau, Joseph, Moses, Rahab, Gideon, Barak, Samson, Jepthah, David and Samuel). The volunteers should study the passage and be prepared to answer the interview questions listed on the handout. (You might also familiarize them with the ideas discussed in the other two options for this section.)

Distribute "Alien Questionnaire" and pens or pencils. Introduce the volunteers, exclaiming: **Can you believe it? We've got Moses over here! And over there, I'd like you to meet Abraham!** (You get the point, right? Ham it up!) Ask students to work in pairs or trios and move around the room, interviewing two of the biblical characters using the questions on the handouts and recording their answers.

After everyone has had a chance to interview two characters, invite students to share what they learned about the Bible characters being aliens and strangers, and how their differences affected their lives. Distribute Bibles and have students read 1 Peter 2:11,12; then discuss the following:

What do you think these verses mean? We're supposed to view life on earth just like those Old Testament believers. Our actions should show that we're people of another culture—the culture of heaven!

Who are the "pagans" the verses refer to? In terms of life today for teens, it means living good lives among people at school who don't know God. Literally, though, there were truly pagan worshipers of other gods in Bible times. Students probably won't know this, though, and that's OK.

Why do you think people would be accused of "doing wrong?" They wouldn't be doing what everyone else was doing.

Invite students to read Galatians 5:16-26; then ask:

What does it look like to put verses 22–26 into practice in your life at school?

If you have time, ask this last question regarding each individual fruit listed in verses 22 and 23.

You'll need Several Bibles.

Distribute Bibles and ask a volunteer to read Hebrews 11:13-16. Discuss:

Why would Abraham, Isaac and the other people mentioned in this passage think of themselves as aliens and strangers? They knew heaven was their real home, and they were just passing through this place called earth.

How do you think that attitude might have changed their relationship with God? It increased their faith, and made them willing to risk their lives on earth for God because they knew they could count on being with Him in heaven. Their hope of living in heaven with God took away their fear of death.

How do you think it might have changed the way they lived? It gave them boldness to live for God, knowing that this place (earth) was just temporary.

Next, have students look at 1 Peter 2:11,12. Ask:

What do you think these verses mean? We're supposed to view life on earth just like those Old Testament believers. Our actions should show that we're people of another culture—the culture of heaven!

Who are the "pagans" the verses refer to? In terms of life today for teens, it means living good lives among people at school who don't know God. Literally, though, there were truly pagan worshipers of other gods in Bible times. Students probably won't know this, though, and that's OK.

Why do you think people would be accused of "doing wrong?" They wouldn't be doing what everyone else was doing.

Invite students to read Galatians 5:16-26; then ask:

What does it look like to put verses 22–26 into practice in your life at school?

If you have time, ask this last question regarding each individual fruit listed in verses 22 and 23.

You'll need Several Bibles, copies of "Alien Outline" (p. 37), pens or pencils and two Barbie- or Ken-type dolls (yes, you really need to bring the dolls!).

Ahead of time, cut the handouts into half-sheets.

The Big Idea

Being a Christian radically changes you.

The Big Question

How does being a Christian make me different from others at my school?

> **Note:** This option has some concepts that are a bit abstract. Students will grasp the concepts much better by using the handout to write down the points as you discuss them.

You're basically going to guide students through a four-step logical approach as to why we should act differently. Be prepared for some attitude when you bring out the dolls to use for making the points of the concept! Many of the students (especially the older ones) will think the use of these dolls is extremely juvenile, unless you goof around with it and make it obvious that you don't think they'd actually still play with these things.

Distribute "Alien Outline" and pens or pencils. Designate one of the dolls to represent the students by claiming: **This doll is *you*! And this one** (the other doll) **represents everyone at school who doesn't know God.** With the right tone of voice and attitude, this will help students to visualize what you're saying.

Use place and distance to represent heaven and earth. For instance, when you talk about being a citizen of heaven, take the Christian (ooh, this could get very weird!) over to one side of the room—designating that area as heaven. When you talk about being a visitor on earth, bring the Christian over to visit the other doll who's on earth. Got it? C'mon, be creative!

Here are the answers to the handout:

As a Christian, you're a *citizen of heaven.*

That makes you a *visitor on earth.*

You should live by the *values of heaven.*

Which means you'll *act differently on earth.*

Distribute Bibles and instruct students to read the following two passages, reflecting on what each says about the idea of being an alien on earth: Hebrews 11:13-16 and 1 Peter 2:11,12.

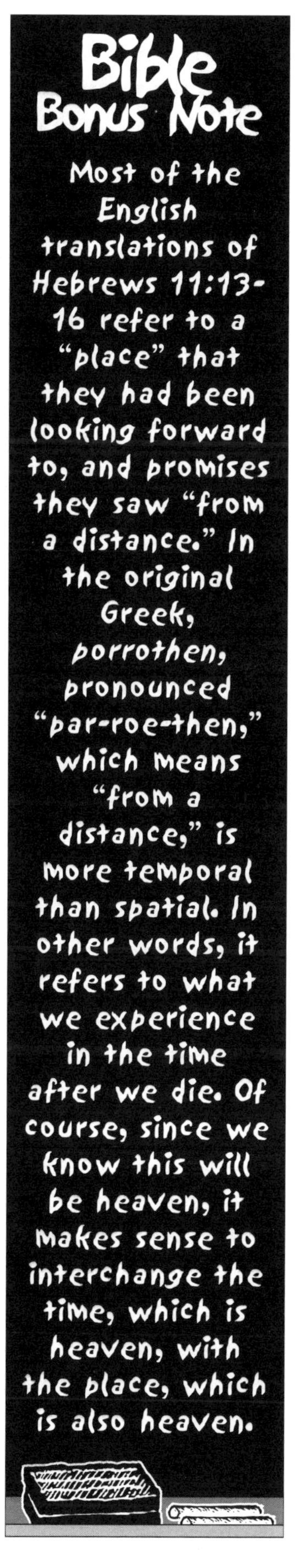

Invite a brief discussion on what acting differently on earth should look like; then read Galatians 5:16-26 and discuss the question some more using verses 22 and 23 for specific alien qualities.

Discuss:

What do you think these verses mean? We're supposed to view life on earth just like those Old Testament believers. Our actions should show that we're people of another culture—the culture of heaven!

Who are the "pagans" the verses refer to? In terms of life today for teens, it means living good lives among people at school who don't know God. Literally, though, there were truly pagan worshipers of other gods in Bible times. Students probably won't know this, though, and that's OK.

Why do you think people would be accused of "doing wrong?" They wouldn't be doing what everyone else was doing.

Invite students to read Galatians 5:16-26; then ask:

What does it look like to put verses 22–26 into practice in your life at school?

If you have time, ask this last question regarding each individual fruit listed in verses 22 and 23.

This step helps students begin to wrestle with the implications of being aliens in their schools.

You'll need A few junior high yearbooks (for added fun, use your own if you still have them).

Ahead of time, copy the pictures in the yearbooks that are the most unusual, funny or even bizarre. If you use students' yearbooks, ask them to select the pictures in advance and explain them to the group.

Show the yearbook pictures and explain that yearbooks are great ways to capture memories of the place where we spend most of our waking hours—school.

Discuss:

How would your life at school be different if you really lived for Christ 100 percent of the time?

What kinds of pictures of you might your yearbook have if you did that?

Have you ever had someone tell you that you seem different?

Was it because of Christ or just because you were being weird?!

Do you know any students at your school who really live for God?

What do they do that makes it obvious that they are Christians?

How would you treat other students if you were really allowing the Holy Spirit to guide your life at school?

How would other students treat you if you acted this way?

What do you think they'd write about you in your yearbook?

How do you feel about being different, about standing out as an alien and a stranger? (For junior highers, the desire to be normal is so great that being alien can be a challenge. Make sure you spend enough time on this question to really let them be honest with their anxiety and fears about being different from others at school. Share your own experiences, even as an adult, where you have been anxious about being an alien.)

You'll need Students who can relate to these case studies.

> **Note:** There are two case studies for this option. Choose one based on the level your students can relate to right now. Both will help them to think about living for God at school.

Case Study #1: Deep

Terrance has just finished lunch and is walking down the hall toward his locker. He hears a voice yelling his name, but can't tell where it's coming from. Out of the crowd squeezes

Cole, a kid in a couple of Terrance's classes. Cole says, "Terrance, I've gotta ask you, what is your deal?"

Terrance, who's a Christian, isn't quite sure what to make of this question and mumbles, "Huh? Did I do something wrong?"

Cole explains, "It's been buggin' me for weeks now. I've been watching you and you are just flat-out *different* from everyone else in this school. I mean, I don't want to be rude or anything, but, like, why are you so different?"

Discuss:

What would you say if you were Terrance?

How might Cole respond?

What kinds of things might Cole have seen Terrance do or say that were different?

Case Study #2: Deeper

Jess was a pretty popular girl—until recently. She made a radical decision a few months ago to totally live for God at school. It was tempting to drop the commitment a whole bunch of times, like when her three best friends told her they didn't want to hang out with her anymore since she wouldn't gossip or do anything fun or when Billy Sheridan started calling her "Jesus freak" all the time. Even the other Christian kids keep their distance from her, saying things like, "You're taking this stuff way too seriously, Jess." You don't go to Jess's school, but you're in her youth group. This afternoon she called and asked you for advice.

Discuss:

What would you say to Jess?

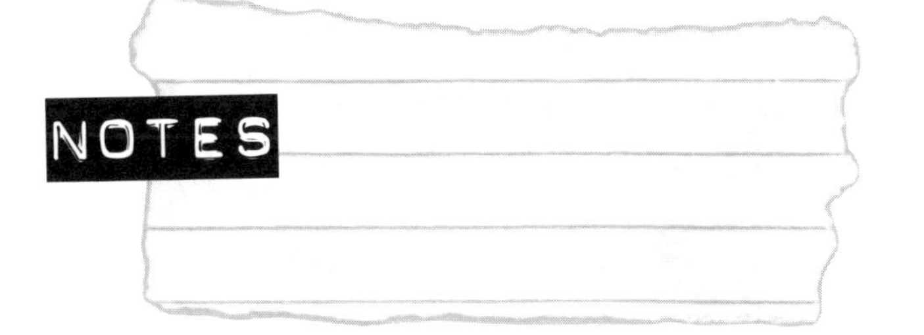

You'll need Zippo, nada, nothing.

1. **How do you know if you're really acting like Christ—or if you're just being weird?** The truth is that lots of people who think they're acting like God would want them to are really just acting dorky. The good news is that we don't have to figure out what it means to act like Christ would want us to on our own. First, we've got the Bible. Second, we've got each other. If you're wondering about how you're acting, and how others are perceiving you, ask someone you respect—a close friend or an adult leader—who you know will tell you the truth.

2. **If God sent Jesus for us to understand Him, and in doing this made Him *more* like us humans, why should we be different? Isn't God's model one of being similar, and not being different?** Although God sent Jesus, His Son, in the form of a human, Jesus was still pretty different. He never sinned, He always loved, and He always said and did the right thing which resulted in much criticism and ultimately His death. So God's model in Jesus is really both similar and different. We're already similar to others around us in that we're human; now we have the chance to show how we're different (see John 17:14-19).

3. **How do you handle it if someone calls you a goody-goody or a Jesus freak or something like that?** On the one hand, there's nothing wrong with being called a Jesus freak for doing the right things. On the other hand, you might be communicating that you feel that you're somehow better than others. The reality is that you're not—you still sin and make mistakes. But you have a relationship with Jesus, and that means that when you blow it you can go to Him and ask forgiveness and make the relationship right. The next time someone calls you a name like that, try to let them know that you make mistakes and blow it, but that you admit it, apologize (if needed) or make things right, and are forgiven.

4. **If I go to church with someone from my school and she acts just like everybody else at school, does that mean she's not a Christian?** That goes back to the definition of Christian: someone who has received Jesus to be his or her Savior and Lord (John 1:12). Receiving Christ changes our hearts and should change our lives, too (Ephesians 5:8). God is the only one who really knows if she has asked Jesus to be her Savior and Lord, but you might want to talk with her about it. If she says that she is a Christian, maybe you and she could talk about what that means and ways that she could be acting differently around school. These might be small baby steps at first, like not making fun of people, throwing away her own trash after lunch or watching her language.

This step helps students choose ways to act differently at school this week.

You'll need Several gift Bibles, a piece of paper and a pen or pencil.

Some students have no reason to be different at school—because they haven't asked Jesus to take over their lives yet. Can you think of anything more important than giving them a chance to do so? As you're explaining the gospel message, you might want to designate one side of your room as God, and the other as Humans, emphasizing the canyon between the two and thus the need for Jesus (the bridge!).

Explain: **We've been talking about how having a relationship with Jesus makes us different. For some of you, this hasn't made much sense because you haven't experienced the most important difference—the difference that motivates us to make all the other kinds of changes we've been talking about. That difference is having a relationship with Jesus.**

Continue: **God is your Creator and loves you more than you can imagine. However, as human beings, we are naturally drawn to do wrong things because our hearts are stained by sin. We will always tend to disobey God's Word and do our own thing instead, and this sin has caused a huge chasm that separates us from God.**

To bridge that chasm of sin, God sent Jesus, His Son, as a human being. Jesus lived a perfectly sinless life here on earth for 33 years and then took the punishment for *our* sins upon Himself when He died on the cross. But that's not the end of the story: Jesus was resurrected, conquering sin and everything else that had separated us from God. Through the sacrifice of His own life He built a bridge for us.

Now you have a choice to make: Confess the sin that separates you from God and receive His gift of salvation or ignore His sacrifice and continue to live under the power of sin. You can ask Jesus to take over your life and help you serve Him every day or try to make the best of life totally on your own. He has made the way; now you must make the decision. Jesus' life, death and resurrection is a bridge between you and God. You must choose whether or not you will cross the bridge and accept Jesus as your Savior and Lord.

Invite students who would like to ask Jesus to come into their lives to pray the following prayer, repeating after you: **Dear Jesus, I know I'm a sinner. I've missed the mark and I feel empty. I need you and I turn my life over to you. Help me to obey you every day and be different from others around me.**

Close by asking students who prayed that prayer for the first time just now to come forward to receive a gift Bible. Congratulate each one on his or her new life in Jesus. Write down names, phone numbers, addresses (e-mail, too!) and contact those students in the coming week to encourage them to become involved with a church (yours or someone else's).

You'll need Copies of "My Alien School" (p. 38) and pens or pencils.

Distribute "My Alien School" and pens or pencils. Ask students to work on their own for a few minutes to write what it would look like to be an "alien for Christ" in their schools. They should list their specific classes in the rooms, and write an action for each class or area. The cafeteria and gym have suggestions already on the handout. The hallway space is for general interaction with friends. Move around the room to make sure they understand what they're supposed to be doing.

After several minutes, pull everyone back together and debrief the time by asking if a few students will share what they've written. Encourage others to add ideas to their sheets if they hear one they missed.

Finally, encourage students to look back over their sheets and circle the actions they'd be willing to risk trying.

Be sure to close this time in prayer, asking God for courage to live as aliens in this strange world called school!

Option 3 Spread the Fire

You'll need Paper and pens or pencils.

If your students are really ready to "go for it" in their commitment to sharing their faith, invite them to make their commitment more firm by writing a letter to someone to tell them about it. The catch? They have to write the letter to one of their teachers. Encourage them to say some nice things about the teacher, and to explain how they're going to try to act in that teacher's class.

Make sure students understand the weight of delivering this letter: If they tell this teacher they're going to represent Christ, but don't follow through, they could hurt the cause of Christ and damage their own credibility.

Close in prayer for the letters and for the teachers that will see Christ in your students.

Alien Questionnaire

Bible Character One: ______________________________

Why did you think of yourself as an alien and a stranger?

How did thinking of yourself as an alien and a stranger affect your actions?

How did others respond to you?

Bible Character Two: ______________________________

Why did you think of yourself as an alien and a stranger?

How did thinking of yourself as an alien and a stranger affect your actions?

How did others respond to you?

Alien Outline

As a Christian, you're a ______________________________

____

That makes you a ______________________________

____

You should live by the ______________________________

____

Which means you'll ______________________________

____

Alien Outline

As a Christian, you're a ______________________________

____

That makes you a ______________________________

____

You should live by the ______________________________

____

Which means you'll ______________________________

____

My Alien School

Think about a typical school day. If you lived as an alien in a foreign land—as a citizen of heaven living by the values of heaven—what would it *look* like in your school? What actions might you do that would be different? (We've already filled in suggestions for gym class and the cafeteria, but feel free to add more!)

CAFETERIA

Inviting a less-than-popular but really nice kid to your table.

ROOM 5

ROOM 1

ROOM 3

ROOM 2

ROOM 4

ROOM 6

Lending a helping hand to kids who don't do so well in gym class.

GYM

OFFICE

Devotions in Motion

Week Two: Alien Invasion!

Quick Questions

Check out Exodus 34:29-35 right here and now.

God Says

What do you think is going to be different about you as a Christian?

- ❑ You'll wear cool Christian T-shirts with Bible verses and little fish on them.
- ❑ You'll carry a 15-pound Bible with you wherever you go.
- ❑ You'll sing "Jesus Loves Me" all day in both English and Spanish.
- ❑ You'll shave your hair in the shape of a cross.

I Do

Some, or all, of those things may be true if you're a Christian. But they don't get at the real issue. They're all things on the outside. The truth is that being a Christian first of all makes you a new creation inside. And as you spend more and more time getting to know and obey God, you'll change on the outside, too. You might not end up glowing like a Christmas tree like Moses did, but the changes will stand out as brightly to everyone around you.

Thank God today that He has changed you, and ask Him to show you other ways He wants to make you different.

FOLD HERE

DAY 4

Fast Facts

Race to 1 Corinthians 4:6,7. I mean it, now—run!

God Says

Betty the Baptist hardly ever talked to Paul the Presbyterian. Sometimes Cathy the Catholic tried to talk to Betty, Paul or even Ephram the Episcopalian and Martin the Methodist, but all they ever talked about was how cool their own youth groups and youth pastors were.

I Do

Although Christians are different from those who don't believe and follow Jesus, we have much in common with each other, regardless of our denominations. Most importantly, we have all received the gift of Jesus, salvation and forgiveness. It's a gift given to you, not a reward you've earned. Jesus has made you different from nonbelievers—not your youth pastor, your church or even your youth group. It's Him!

Pray today for other Christians you know at your school who don't go to your church. Ask God to help you all love and serve each other, and who knows—others around you just might notice!

FasT FacTs

Flip open ThaT There Bible To Luke 6:27-31.

God Says

Maria really bugs you. Every day she asks To borrow 50 cenTs for lunch and she never even Thanks you for lending iT To her—or pays you back. She never does her science homework, Then asks you every Thursday during lunch To copy yours. AT leasT once a week she borrows a pen, buT she never gives iT back.

Now Maria has really gone Too far. She's Telling people ThaT you said some mean Things abouT Kim, buT all you ever said was ThaT you were Too Tired To go over To Kim's house afTer school.

I Do

WhaT you really wanT To do is yell aT Maria or sTop leTTing her borrow any money. You're TempTed To Tell everyone whaT a leech she is Too. Jesus painTs a differenT picTure, Though. He asks you To love people who are your enemies, which includes people who hurT you or say mean Things abouT you. In Maria's case, This mighT mean simply puTTing a liTTle disTance beTween you and her or noT leTTing her borrow sTuff all The Time. The imporTanT Thing is ThaT Jesus sTill wanTs you To pray for her and be her friend.

Is There anybody who is bugging you? Like a broTher, a neighbor, a Teacher or anoTher kid aT school? Spend a few minuTes praying for ThaT person Today, asking God To give you compassion for ThaT person.

FOLD HERE

Quick QuesTions

Use Those sharp eyes of yours To read John 9:13-34.

God Says

If you knew a way ThaT everybody could geT a million dollars (yourself included), how would you spread The news?

- ❑ GeT your own web page wiTh some cool links To oTher siTes.
- ❑ RenT a blimp and drop birds from iT ThaT have messages sTrapped around Their neck.
- ❑ Learn how To fly a plane and Tie a sign behind iT wiTh informaTion on how To geT The money.
- ❑ Dress up like a dollar bill and sTand on a corner.

I Do

IT's amazing how, when you have good news, you'll do anyThing To share iT. The same was True when Jesus healed The man's blindness in John 9:13-34. The man wanTed To share iT wiTh his neighbors.

You've goT The incredible news ThaT Jesus offers a new life and new hope To everybody you know. He's made you differenT and He's ready and waiTing To make oThers you know differenT, Too.

Spend Two minuTes praying for Two people ThaT you know who haven'T yeT leT Jesus make a difference in Their lives.

SESSIONTHREESESSIONTHREESESSIONTHREE

Through and Through

The Big Idea

Following Christ means living a life of integrity everywhere, including school.

Session Aims

In this session you will guide students to:

- Learn what integrity is;
- Think about their own integrity—or lack of it—especially in school;
- Make a plan to increase their integrity at school this week.

The Biggest Verse

"The man of integrity walks securely, but he who takes crooked paths will be found out." Proverbs 10:9

"Don't let anyone look down on you because you are young, but set an example for the believers in speech, in life, in love, in faith and in purity." 1 Timothy 4:12

Other Important Verses

Proverbs 10:9; 11:3; Mark 12:13-17; 1 Timothy 4:12

This step helps students define integrity.

You'll need Sturdy chairs for students!

Ahead of time, arrange the chairs in rows like you might find in a classroom.

Welcome students and ask: **What is integrity?** When something or someone is what it is—nothing to hide, nothing fake.

Continue: **I'm going to read a list of statements, along with a direction of movement and the number of seats to move. If this statement is true of you, you have to move that number and direction of seats. If someone is in that seat, sit on his or her lap. If two or more people are stacked on that seat, sit on them. If you get to the end of a row, circle back to the other end.**

Read the following list, pausing after each statement for students to move:

If you've ever . . .

- **lied about anything at school, move one seat to the right.**
- **cheated on a test or quiz, move two seats to the left.**
- **been nice to someone only so they would be nice to you, move one seat forward.**
- **made up a fake excuse about homework you didn't do, move three seats to the right.**
- **copied the answers to homework from someone else, move two seats backward.**
- **asked to be excused to the restroom when you didn't actually have to go, move four seats to the left.**
- **taken something from someone else's lunch when they weren't looking, move one seat forward.**
- **pretended to know what you were doing when you didn't, move two seats to the right.**
- **lied to the principal or assistant principal, move three seats backward.**
- **pretended to be sick so you didn't have to go to school, move five seats to the left.**
- **pretended to be hurt so you didn't have to participate in gym class, move two seats to the right.**
- **lacked integrity, go back to your original seat.**

Wrap up by stating: **We all lack integrity sometimes, but as followers of Jesus Christ we're called on to live lives of integrity even at work or school.**

You'll need Enough bittersweet baking chocolate (found in the baking supplies aisle of your local grocery store) and milk chocolate to give students a piece of each.

Greet students and explain that you have a special treat today. Distribute the bittersweet chocolate (don't let on that it's baking chocolate) and instruct students to wait until everyone has a piece to eat it. After everyone has a piece, invite them to eat it and be ready for some protesting about the taste! Distribute the real chocolate as you explain: **Things are often different than they appear to be at first. The same is true with people.** Discuss the following questions, making sure students know not to mention anyone by name when answering:

Do you know anyone who pretends to be someone he or she isn't?

What or who did that person pretend to be?

Have you ever known someone who said one thing, but did the opposite?

What did he or she do that was different from what he or she said?

What is it called when someone does that? Hypocrisy.

What's integrity? It's possible that students will be familiar with the word, but not really know what it means. Explain that it's the things you just talked about: not being hypocritical, not pretending to be someone you're not, etc. It's walking securely in who you are.

How does integrity relate to being an example? If you have integrity, you'll automatically be an example to people, especially to students at school who aren't used to being around people with integrity.

Sum up: **Today we're going to figure out how you can have integrity and be an example to the people you hang out with at school.**

You'll need One copy of "I Said It—I'll Do It" (p. 50) and a hat, box or bag. **Optional:** Candy for the winning team.

Ahead of time, cut the handout into individual slips and place the slips into the hat.

> **Note:** If your group is typically large or if you plan to play several rounds of the game, cut three or four copies of the handout into strips and place all of them into the hat.

Divide students into at least three teams; then ask each team to send a representative forward. One at a time, each representative will select a slip from the hat and read his or her action out loud. When everyone has selected an action, all of the representatives must perform the action they selected and read out loud. Award 100 points to those who perform their tasks to your satisfaction.

Play as many rounds as you have time for and award a prize to the team with the most points at the end. (If you opted not to get the candy for prizes, don't worry! The prize of warm admiration of the rest of the group can be a great thing, too!)

Oh, and in case you didn't catch it, the point of this game is following through on what you say you'll do: a key component to integrity. After all, it's easy to talk the talk, but it's not always easy to walk the talk!

After the game is over, discuss:

What is integrity? When something or someone is what it is—nothing to hide, nothing fake.

How does integrity relate to being an example? If we have integrity, we'll automatically be a good example to people, especially to students at school who aren't used to being around people with integrity.

What does following through have to do with integrity? Everything! If someone claims to have integrity, and doesn't do as he or she says, that person is lying and being a poor example.

Youth Leader Tip

Points are free! We youth leaders can sometimes be awfully stingy when it comes to giving out points in competition. Have you ever asked yourself why? The reason for using a competitive game in teaching is for fun and educational value, not for winning and losing. So go crazy with points! If a team does well, give 'em 100 points, 1,000 points—3,278 points! If everyone's getting 100 points for a "correct" answer, but someone does it with gusto—give him or her an extra 25 points. If someone completes the letter of the law, but not the spirit of the law, only give him or her 50 or 75 points. Give extra points for creativity, supportiveness, good attitude, pain—whatever. Take points away for mocking another team or contestant, complaining, cheating, bad attitude, etc. Make the third and fourth rounds of play worth more points so losing teams have an opportunity to catch up. Remember: The point is to have fun!

This step helps students understand how to be a model of integrity.

You'll need Several Bibles and a copy of "Multiple-Choice Melodramas" (p. 51).

Recruit four volunteers to act in a set of three melodramas. (Be sure to select students who will actually play the parts, not just sidetrack the exercise into something else!) Assign one person the role of Jesus (someone who won't turn the melodramas into complete blasphemy!) and three students the roles of the Pharisees. Instruct the Pharisees to sit together, in the middle of the rest of the students (the crowd).

Explain that the melodramas they will be acting out are all based on the same Bible story. Characters should act out their parts as you read them and if there's a line to be spoken, the character should just repeat it after you read it.

When all the melodramas have been acted out, ask students to vote on which one was closest to the real Bible story. Before you reveal the correct answer (which, by the way, is version three), distribute Bibles and have everyone turn to Mark 12:13-17. Read the real story aloud; then discuss:

Why did the Pharisees begin by mentioning that they knew Jesus was a man of integrity? They were attempting to flatter Him because they were getting ready to trap Him, and wanted to prove that He didn't have integrity. Of course, Jesus didn't need their flattery—His integrity was never a question to Him.

Why did they ask Him the question about taxes? (It's unlikely that students will know the answer, but ask anyway—you may be pleasantly surprised!) The Romans required the Jews to pay tribute money into the emperor's treasury. Some Jews—like the Zealots—refused to pay; some—like the Pharisees—disliked paying, but usually did it anyway; and some—like the Herodians—had no objection to paying.

The question was intended to trap Jesus. In their view, He only had two options in answering—that the people should pay taxes or that they shouldn't. Neither answer would be right because the first would offend many of the Jews by going against Jesus' teachings that everything belonged to God; the second answer would have placed Jesus in a dangerous position against the Roman government, which would prove that He didn't have integrity.

How did Jesus' answer show that He had integrity? He surprised them with His answer that some things belonged to Caesar. The meaning behind His answer was: Sure, pay your *taxes* as you should to Caesar, but everything you have and are belongs to God. Jesus' whole life showed that He lived up to this standard of putting God first and *then* taking care of your responsibilities to others.

Youth Leader Tip

Although the principle that we want to make sure students understand about integrity and setting an example in school is taught in 1 Timothy 4:12, junior highers seem to remember stories more than anything else. That's why this lesson weaves together Paul's writings and Proverbs with a story about Jesus. Anytime you can tie a narrative from Scripture into a principle or verse from the Epistles, you're sure to maximize students' comprehension and memory of what you discuss with them.

Read Proverbs 10:9 and ask: **How did Jesus' actions and words help make His walk secure?** Since He always did the right thing, He knew that God would be pleased with His steps.

Close by reading 1 Timothy 4:12 aloud; then discuss:

How does this verse relate to integrity? Paul wrote of setting an example.

Do you think age makes a difference in practicing integrity? No, people of any age can choose to live with or without integrity; but the earlier you make it a practice, the better for you and your Christian witness.

Since Paul mentioned "speech," "life," "love," "faith" and "purity," is there anything he left out? No! These are the keys to integrity.

You'll need Several Bibles.

Distribute Bibles as you explain the setting of the story: **Jesus was teaching about giving yourself completely to God; and the Pharisees, who were already angered by Him** (see Mark 11:15-18), **wanted to trap Him by showing He didn't have integrity.** Have students follow along while you read Mark 12:13-17; then discuss:

Why did the Pharisees begin by mentioning that they knew Jesus was a man of integrity? They were attempting to flatter Him because they were preparing to trap Him, and wanted to prove that He didn't have integrity. Of course, Jesus didn't need their flattery—His integrity was never a question to Him.

How was this trap supposed to work? (This is a tough one, so don't be surprised if no one yells out the answer.) The Romans required the Jews to pay tribute money to the emperor's treasury. Some Jews—like the Zealots—refused to pay; some—like the Pharisees—disliked paying, but usually did it anyway; and some—like the Herodians—had no objection to paying.

The question was intended to trap Jesus. In their view, He only had two options in answering—that the people should pay taxes or that they shouldn't. Neither answer would be right because the first would offend many of the Jews by supporting the Gentile/Roman government; the second answer would have placed Jesus in a dangerous position against the Roman government, which would prove that He didn't have integrity.

Why didn't the trap work? For a couple of reasons: first, Jesus was smarter than that, and second, because He *had* integrity. His answers weren't meant to be tricky, and He'd really meant everything He'd said up to that point about giving yourself to God.

How did Jesus' actions show that He had integrity? (This isn't an easy question; let students wrestle with it for a bit before explaining the answer.) Jesus lived out what He said. He wasn't trying to overthrow Caesar or take what belonged to Caesar—but He meant what He said when He taught that everything belongs to God, and He showed that He meant it with His life—even to the point of dying on the Cross.

Read Proverbs 10:9 and discuss:

How did Jesus' actions and words help make His walk secure? Since He always did the right thing, He knew that God would be pleased with His steps.

What other things did Jesus do during His life that showed He had integrity? See what your students can come up with!

Bible Bonus Note

Mark 12:13 mentions two groups approaching Jesus: Pharisees and Herodians. These two groups disliked each other. The Pharisees were the keepers of the law and totally opposed to Caesar's rule; the Herodians were also influential Jewish leaders who supported Caesar's and Herod's rule. Normally opposed to each other, they had one thing in common: both were threatened by Jesus and wanted Him out of the picture. For this reason, they banded together through a common bond to trap Jesus with His answer.

Close by reading 1 Timothy 4:12 and discussing:

How does this verse relate to integrity? Paul wrote of setting an example.

Do you think age makes a difference in practicing integrity? No, people of any age can choose to live with or without integrity; but the earlier you make it a habit, the better for you and your Christian witness.

Since Paul mentions "speech," "life," "love," "faith" and "purity," is there anything he leaves out? No, although students might try to add something. When they make additional suggestions, have them decide in which category their suggestions might fit.

How did Jesus set an example in these five areas? Have students think of stories where Jesus demonstrated integrity in these five areas.

How can we set examples in these five areas? Students' answers will vary.

You'll need Your Bible, a piece of plastic fruit and a real piece of the same kind of fruit.

The Big Idea

Like Jesus, Christians are called to have integrity.

The Big Question

How do we live lives of integrity?

1. Having integrity means you are what you say you are, and you mean what you say.

Hold up the plastic piece of fruit and state: **This is an orange** (or apple, banana, etc.). Hold up the real fruit: ***This* is an orange, too. So what's the difference? Obviously, one's *really* an orange and one is just *pretending* to be an orange. The same is true for people. Some people say they're honest, but really aren't. Some people make a commitment to do something or be somewhere, but don't follow through. Some people say they're followers of Christ, but don't really live like Jesus at all. Jesus showed His integrity all the time. One great example is in Mark 12:13-17.** Read the passage; then ask the questions at the end of Option 1.

2. Integrity isn't proven by what you say; it's proven by what you do.

Explain that the *saying* part only sets us up to prove whether or not we have integrity. It's in the *doing* that the proof shows up. Hold up the plastic fruit again and explain: **A person might not realize this isn't an orange until she held it or tried to bite into it. The same is true for all of us—just as it was true for Jesus. He proved his integrity with His life. We also prove our integrity by how we live our lives, by being honest, by not cheating, by following through on commitments and by not trying to act like someone else.** Read 1 Timothy 4:12 aloud; then explain that the five ways to set an example of integrity—speech, life, love, faith and purity—sum up what it means to *have* integrity in each of these areas.

This step turns the corner and helps students apply integrity to their school lives.

You'll need Dis book, see?

> **Option:** This could be a great small-group opportunity. Divide students into groups of four or five. Give a different situation to each group to explore together. Have them share their answers to each situation.

Read the following situations one at a time, pausing between each to ask these questions:

What would this person have to do in order to have integrity?

What might be the consequences in this situation if he or she doesn't have integrity?

What if he or she *does* have integrity? Make sure students think of tangible consequences (e.g., do better or worse on homework, be made fun of or be accepted by others) as well as less tangible ones (e.g., feeling guilty, feeling upset, feeling peaceful).

Situation One:

Megan really wants to be accepted. And it seems like she can be accepted if she acts like a flirty airhead because all those girls at school get a lot of attention.

Situation Two:

Mike has to do a history project with Sam. And Sam is supersmart and very willing to do all the work. Mike agreed to research a certain part of their project. But he knows Sam will do it without complaining.

Situation Three:

Sarah's friend Jessie knows the answer Sarah can't remember on the test. And Jessie has her paper where Sarah can see it. Sarah knows Jessie wouldn't mind if she peeked, and the teacher is helping another student at the front of the room and couldn't possibly see her.

Situation Four:

Phil did a stupid thing—he accidentally started a rumor about his friend Zack. When Zack asks him if he started it, Phil could easily say no and get away with it.

You'll need Just this story about good ol' Jerod and the questions that follow.

Use this case study and the following questions for discussion:

Jerod is frustrated. He wants to live totally for Jesus. But he knows that means he has to live like Jesus would want him to at school—and that means no cheating at all. He's gotten into such a habit of cheating that he doesn't know how he can stop. All the kids at school do it—even the other Christians. And it's so *easy*. His teachers never catch him, and no one's bugging him about it—except Jesus! It's not like anyone's come up to him and said, "Jerod, I can't believe in Jesus because *you* don't have integrity."

Discuss:

What would you say to Jerod?

So what if he cheats a little; who's it going to hurt?

What if he just doesn't cheat quite as often?

You'll need Students who are ready for a meatier question/discussion option!

1. **What does it mean to have integrity?** It means being truthful, being trustworthy, doing what you say you will do—even when it is difficult.

2. **Why is it hard to have integrity at school?** Because so many people around you don't have integrity or they don't even know what it is or that it is important. Many people don't even know someone who demonstrates integrity. Just as Jesus was criticized, His followers will be, too. Yet He promises blessings when we are obedient to Him.

3. **What do you do if having integrity in a situation means you'll make someone mad, such as when you tell the truth and a friend gets in trouble?** Try to do everything you can to help him or her understand why you're doing what you're doing, like talking with him or her about it before or after you act. But you can't let others' responses control how you act. Jesus didn't, did He?

4. **What do you do if having integrity in a situation will get you in trouble?** This is tough to say, but having integrity is much more valuable than the cost of the trouble. Nothing is worth losing your integrity—not even being grounded or losing a friendship.

5. **What might be some of the negative consequences of having integrity all the time without any exceptions?** You could make some friends mad at you; you might have to reveal stuff about yourself you'd rather keep secret; you might have to really be yourself when you'd rather put on an act; and you might have to tell the truth when a little lie would sure be easier.

This step helps students some decisions about their own integrity.

You'll need Copies of "My Integrity" (p. 52) and pens or pencils.

Distribute "My Integrity" and pens or pencils. Allow a few minutes for students to complete the handouts; then discuss their answers as a group. After the discussion, close in prayer, asking for the Holy Spirit's guidance and strength to live with integrity this coming week.

Note: If your group is large, this would be best accomplished in smaller groups with an adult leader in each group.

You'll need Your Bible, 3x5-inch index cards and pens or pencils.

If students are really excited about having integrity, explain that all of us show a lack of integrity from time to time. Explain: **One of the signs of real integrity is to make right the areas where we've lacked integrity.** Read 1 John 1:8—2:1 and discuss the truth that although we all sin, we have a way out—Jesus! Summarize: **When we confess our sins, He forgives us and cleanses us. We aren't just trying to "be good" or "do better next time"; with His power and help we can change and grow in our ability to act with integrity.**

Distribute the index cards and ask students to write down one time in the past two weeks when they lacked integrity and weren't good examples to others around them.

Note: It's almost always easier for students to be open and honest about their own struggles when you volunteer an example from your own life first.

Instruct students to turn their cards over and write a plan of action for turning their experiences lacking integrity into a situation where integrity would be shown. This is a very gutsy thing to do, and will take great courage on the part of students. Close in prayer, asking God to guide each student through his or her plan of action.

You'll need Students would be a great addition to this option!

Explain: **A person's degree of integrity speaks loudly about his or her relationship with Jesus—and believe it or not, others are listening!**

Ask for two volunteers to come forward. Share the following scenario:

> **You are a Christian and you're caught cheating on your science test. Your teacher asks you to stay after class. Sitting right next to you is your non-Christian friend, Juanita, who you've been trying to witness to all year. During lunch, Juanita asks you why you cheated, especially since you're a Christian.**

At this point, assign the role of the Christian to one of the volunteers and the role of Juanita to the other. Let them know that they're going to continue the story in character by talking to each other. If an audience member wants to participate at any point, he or she should yell "Freeze!" The actors will stop and the audience member will take the place of the character he or she chooses and resume the dialogue.

Explain: **It might sound strange, but whenever people realize that we aren't perfect just because we're Christians it gives us chances to share about Jesus with them. After all, if we were perfect, we wouldn't need Jesus, right? We need Him not only for our salvation, but for every day after that, to give us the strength and desire to do the right thing.**

Invite students to pray silently for someone in their lives who needs to understand his or her need for Jesus. Allow 30 to 60 seconds of silent prayer; then close with a prayer asking Jesus to help students use their relationship with Him in a way that will bring others to Him.

I Said It—I'll Do It

I will run up to someone and give him or her a bear hug.

I will run around like a chicken.

I will sing the national anthem.

I will pretend to play in a championship Ping-Pong match with an imaginary friend.

I will recite a poem of my own creation.

I will rub my stomach and pat my head at the same time.

I will impersonate the teacher or youth leader.

I WILL PERFORM A DISCO DANCE.

I will be a tiger—a big mean one!

I will impersonate an auctioneer.

I will Tickle someone.

I WILL IMPERSONATE A POPULAR SINGER.

I will be a chimpanzee showing off in a zoo.

I will act like I'm dying.

Multiple-Choice Melodramas

Version One

Jesus was teaching a bunch of people about something important. The people were listening and nodding and making noises of agreement. Then three Pharisees raised their hands, and asked, in unison: "Hey Jesus, what's integrity?" The crowd was silent, with their mouths open, waiting for Jesus' response. Jesus answered, "Integrity is being the same, through and through." The crowd knew that the Pharisees did not have integrity, so they pointed at them and laughed loudly, while shouting, "No integrity! No integrity!"

Version Two

Jesus was teaching a bunch of people about something important. The people were listening and nodding and making noises of agreement. Then three Pharisees stood up in the middle of the crowd and yelled, "Hey Jesus!" The crowd was shocked and made that very obvious. They started yelling at the Pharisees, "Sit down!" and "Be quiet!" Jesus silenced the crowd, and then turned to the Pharisees. "Do you have a question?" He asked. They said, in perfect unison: "Who is Caesar?" The crowd groaned. Jesus answered, "He's the guy whose face is on coins." The crowd roared with laughter and approval, and a few of them chased the Pharisees away.

Version Three

Jesus was teaching a bunch of people about something important. The people were listening and nodding and making noises of agreement. Then three Pharisees stood up and said, "Jesus, we know you are a man of integrity." The crowd was hushed, waiting with eagerness to see what would happen next. A couple of them were so eager they fell off their chairs! The Pharisees continued, "Is it right to pay taxes to Caesar or not?" Now the crowd was even more eager, because they knew almost any answer Jesus gave could get Him in trouble. A couple more members of the crowd fell off their chairs with eagerness. Jesus looked at their coins and calmly asked, "Whose portrait is this? And whose inscription?" The Pharisees answered, "Caesar's." Jesus continued, "Give to Caesar what is Caesar's and to God what is God's." The Pharisees knew they hadn't trapped Jesus, and left the room muttering and sputtering and whining. The crowd, amazed at Jesus' wisdom, gasped in perfect unison.

My Integrity

Part One

Rewrite these verses in your own words:

Proverbs 10:9

"The man of integrity walks securely, but he who takes crooked paths will be found out."

Proverbs 11:3

"The integrity of the upright guides them, but the unfaithful are destroyed by their duplicity."

Part Two

What would these two verses mean if you applied them to your life at school this week?

Part Three

What's one specific act of integrity that you can do this week?

Devotions in Motion

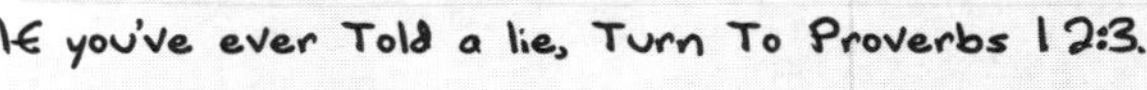

Week Three: Through and Through

DAY 1

Fast Facts

If you've ever Told a lie, Turn To Proverbs 12:3.

God Says

Lynda hated it when her mom made her go over To Laura's house. The only reason she had To go was because her mom was friends with Laura's stepmom. Lynda Thought Laura was Totally boring, and her house had nothing fun To do in it. Laura's family didn't have cable TV and only kept health food around The house.

On Thursday afternoon, Lynda's mom asked her To come over To Laura's house for a few hours. Lynda didn't want To go so she lied and said she didn't feel well. Her mom believed her and decided To stay home with her in case she started feeling worse.

About 20 minutes later, Lynda got a phone call from Carl, a guy from church That she liked. He invited Lynda To go skateboarding with him and Erika and James. Lynda raced downstairs To ask her mom if she could go. Her mom said, "I'm sorry, honey, but not This Time. After all, you said you weren't feeling well."

I Do

One of The big problems with lying is That we have To keep lying To cover our Tracks. Another big problem is That no one will believe us later when we are Telling The Truth. Lynda felt just fine. She would have had no problem skateboarding, but her mom didn't believe her and so she didn't get To go. This proves That it's better To Tell The Truth in The first place.

Ask God To help you Tell The Truth This week, even if your first Thought is To Tell a lie instead.

FOLD HERE

DAY 4

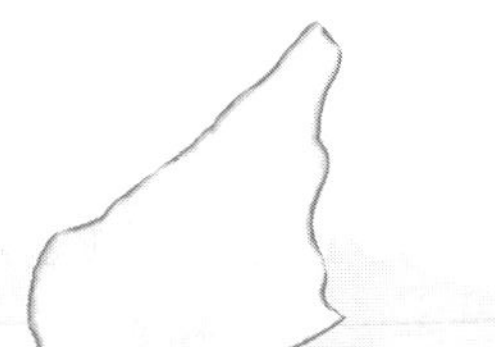

Quick Questions

If you've ever wondered what To do with your money, check out Luke 16:13.

God Says

If you got $20 from your grandma for your birthday, what would you do with it?

- ❑ Spend it all on That new blue shirt you've been eyeing all month.
- ❑ Put it all in The bank so That you'd make more money.
- ❑ Give 10 percent To The church and spend The remaining $18 on a new CD.
- ❑ Hide it in your secret piggy bank.

I Do

One way That our integrity is put To The Test is with our money. How do you handle your money? Do you give 10 percent of it back To God? After all, He gave you 100 percent of it To begin with. If you let money or Things control you, you'll have a harder Time understanding That God is in control.

Do you need To give more of your money away or possibly give more To The church? Ask God Today To show you what To do.

Quick Questions

If you care about what people think about you, read Proverbs 19:1.

God Says

What do you want people to say about you behind your back?

- ❑ You are good-looking.
- ❑ You are fun to be with.
- ❑ You do the right thing.
- ❑ You have the coolest after-school snacks at your place.

I Do

Any of those things would be okay, but if you could choose only one, the best one would be that you do the right thing. According to Proverbs 19:1, it's really best to make good steps and have a blameless walk.

Today you're probably going to have some choices to make about how to act. Ask God to show you how to do the right thing, even if it won't be easy (and to be honest, chances are it won't be).

FOLD HERE

DAY 3

Fast Facts

If you'd like to stay safe, check out Psalm 25:21.

God Says

All the kids in Natalie's group were going out to smash mailboxes on Halloween. Natalie wanted to hang out with her friends, and boy, was she tempted to go, but she knew deep inside that it wouldn't be the right thing to do.

The day after Halloween, Natalie called her friend Paige to see how it went. Paige's mom answered the phone and wouldn't let Natalie talk to Paige. Natalie asked, "Is something wrong?" Paige's mom answered, "You should be glad you weren't with Paige and her friends last night. They were arrested for vandalism when they were caught destroying people's mailboxes. Paige won't be talking to anyone on the phone—or doing much of anything, for that matter—for a while."

I Do

Doing the right thing protects you from all sorts of bad stuff. Sure, you might not get to do everything your friends are doing, but you won't get in trouble (at least as much trouble) and you'll know down deep inside that you're making the right decisions.

Ask God to help you make right choices today. Who knows? Your friends might even follow your choices!

SESSIONFOURSESSIONFOURSESSIONFOUR

The Big Idea

Everything you say about others should help—not hurt—them.

Session Aims

In this session you will guide students to:

- Learn what gossip is—and what it isn't;
- Understand what it feels like to have someone gossip about them;
- Write a commitment to God to move away from gossip.

Have You Heard?

The Biggest Verse

"If anyone considers himself religious and yet does not keep a tight rein on his tongue, he deceives himself and his religion is worthless." James 1:26

Other Important Verses

Proverbs 11:13; 16:28; 18:8; 20:19; 26:20; 2 Corinthians 12:20; James 1:26; 3:5,6

This step gets students thinking about gossip, how it works, and its effects.

You'll need One copy of "Rumor Slips" (p. 63) for every eight students. **Optional:** A life-size drawing of an anonymous young teen (someone students wouldn't know) or picture of one on an overhead or Power Point slide. The teen could have a name tag with "Hello, my name is Chris" written on it.

Ahead of time, cut the handout into individual slips of paper and fold them in half. **Option for 30 or more students:** Group students according to the rumor they received and allow one minute to strategize how they'll spread their rumors to the whole group.

> **Note:** This game will be tough with fewer than 11 students. It's still possible, but you'll need to do some heavy modification. If there's no time for that, use Option 2 or 3 instead.

Greet students and as you distribute the rumor slips, inform them that they are each being given a rumor about a make-believe teen named Chris. Stress that students must keep the information they receive about Chris to themselves until the game begins.

When you give the signal, students are to pair off and ask each other, "What have you heard about Chris?"; then each partner will whisper the rumor he or she has on his or her rumor slip. When you give the signal again, students will switch partners and whisper their own rumors and the ones they were just told. Repeat the process four times; then ask students to return to their seats. Read the rumors out loud one at a time. Those who heard a particular rumor should raise their hands and say, "I heard that!" This isn't really a competition (though you could play it as such); you're just goofing around to see which rumors spread the most.

Transition to the next step by explaining: **Life at school is often like this. Rumors get spread and people like Chris get hurt. Today we're going to check out what the Bible has to say about rumors and gossip and decide how that might make a difference in the way we act at school.**

You'll need A phone booth, a red cape and the ability to leap tall buildings in a single bound. OK, OK . . . just kiddin'. All you need is this book!

Greet students and let them know you have some big news to share about a certain member in the youth group (or a favorite celebrity). Drop a name of someone well-known and popular in the group whose name would pique the rest of the group's interest. Hint that the news is some really juicy gossip; then explain that you probably shouldn't tell. See if they'll begin to put pressure on you to share. Explain that you don't really have some news, but that you wanted to see how they would respond if you really had some gossip to share.

Discuss:

What is gossip? Sharing information about someone—or even a group of people—when the information doesn't need to be shared.

How often does someone try to share gossip with you? Once a week? Once a day? Several times a day? Lots of times a day?

Why is gossip so much fun? We often make ourselves feel better by talking down about other people; we like secrets. (Allow students to come up with several answers on this one.)

How did you feel when you thought I had some big news to share with you today?

How can gossip hurt people?

Have you ever been hurt by gossip?

Transition to the next step by explaining that gossip almost always hurts people, and that's probably one of the reasons the Bible has so much to say about it.

You'll need Paper, pens or pencils and a candy prize for the winning team.

Ahead of time, write down a sentence that would be

easily garbled by the time it's passed from person to person down a line, so that the last person in the line wouldn't necessarily hear the same phrase you spoke to the first person. If you can't come up with one, here's a suggestion: *The frog jumped on the top of the metal roof at 12:00, counted 11 stars and 9 planets, skipped to the aluminum chimney and slid down the bronze rain gutter.*

Select an impartial judge for the game; then divide the rest of the group into teams of 10 students each. **Option for smaller groups:** It will be difficult to set this up as a competition with fewer than 11 students, so it can also be played with one team in a noncompetitive format.

Have the teams form lines and distribute a piece of paper and a pen or pencil to the person at the end of each team's line; then explain that students are going to compete in a test of their gossip ability. You'll whisper a sentence into the ear of the first person on each team; then that person will turn and whisper into the next person's ear and so on down the line. The last person to hear the sentence will write it, exactly as he or she heard it, on a blank piece of paper—not letting anyone see it. The impartial judge will keep track of the time from when you begin whispering the sentence to when the last person is done writing the sentence.

Scoring is as follows: The team that completes the task in the shortest amount of time receives 100 points. The second place team receives 75 points and so on, reducing the points by 25 for each subsequent place. After you read the original sentence aloud, the students at the end of each line will read what they've written on their papers. The impartial judge will award between 0 and 75 points to each team for accuracy.

Total the points and award the candy to the winning team. Transition to the next step by pointing out: **This same thing frequently happens at school. A rumor starts, and by the end of the day, it's been totally blown out of proportion. Today we're going to see how you can act radically different when you hear rumors and gossip at school.**

This step shows students what the Bible has to say about gossip.

You'll need Several Bibles and some students!

Read the following verse pairings from Proverbs. In each pair, the verse with an asterisk is the real verse and the other verse is, well, slightly modified. *Don't tell students which is the correct verse.* When you read the first verse in each pair, point to one wall in the room. When you read the second verse in the pair, point to the opposing wall.

Youth Leader Tip

As the facilitator of your group's discussions, your role is to embrace an attitude of honesty and transparency. This is tricky with junior highers—striking a balance between not being honest and transparent enough (on one extreme) and being so honest and transparent about your own weakness (on the other extreme) that students see in you an excuse for sinning. The topic of gossip is perfect for applying this principle. Allow students to see that you struggle with it, too—after all, everyone does—and you'll create an atmosphere where they'll be more willing to look at this sin in their own lives.

Instruct students to move to the wall that they think represents the real verse. Oh, and by the way, these will be very easy—but that's OK. They have educational value, as the false verse presents false messages and assumptions; and it's fun for students to be right anyhow!

Proverbs 11:13

***A gossip betrays a confidence, but a trustworthy man keeps a secret.**

Everyone gossips, so be careful what secrets you share.

Proverbs 16:28

Gossip can destroy friendships, but sometimes it's just too fun to avoid.

***A perverse man stirs up dissension, and a gossip separates close friends.**

Proverbs 18:8

***The words of a gossip are like choice morsels; they go down to a man's inmost parts.**

Gossip just goes in one ear and out the other—it doesn't really affect you.

Proverbs 20:19

***A gossip betrays a confidence; so avoid a man who talks too much.**

Just because someone gossips to you all the time doesn't mean they'll gossip about you to someone else.

Proverbs 26:20

***Without wood a fire goes out; without gossip a quarrel dies down.**

If you gossip about a friend you're fighting with, it could help end the fight.

Once everyone is seated, distribute Bibles and point out that it's not just the Old Testament that talks about gossip. Read 2 Corinthians 12:20 aloud; then ask for a volunteer to read James 1:26. Discuss:

What does it mean to keep a "tight rein" on your tongue? Hold it back, to not say the first thing that comes to your mind.

How does James link the tongue and religion? If you bad-mouth others, your religion is worthless.

Do you think this is true?

Does that mean if you spread gossip and rumors that you're not a Christian? Since junior highers think so concretely (in black-and-white terms), point out that what makes a person a Christian is receiving Jesus as Savior and Lord. The "religion" that James refers to in 1:26 are outward acts for show, rather than from an actual relationship with God through Christ. In other words, gossip can destroy your credibility as a Christian witness to others.

Option 2 Chat Room

You'll need Several Bibles, a watch or clock with a seconds indicator, candy for prizes, a large sheet of paper and a pen or pencil.

Ahead of time, write the following words on the paper: "anger," "jealousy," "arrogance," "afraid" and "gossip."

Ask for four volunteers and pair them up. Send one team out of the room (you might want to send an adult leader with them to make sure no one wanders down to the corner donut shop). Give one of the remaining team members the paper with the list, instructing him or her to keep the list a secret. The student with the list is the Talker and his or her teammate is the Guesser. The Talker will describe the words, one at a time, to the Guesser while you (or another adult) keep track of how long it takes for the Guesser to get all five words exactly correct (e.g., "angry" isn't good enough; it has to be "anger"). When all the words have been guessed, bring in the other team, designate one teammate as the Talker and one as the Guesser, and repeat the whole process. Award the candy prize to the team that guesses the words in the shortest amount of time.

Distribute Bibles while you explain that Paul used all five of these words in one powerful sentence. Select a volunteer to read 2 Corinthians 12:20; then discuss:

What is quarreling? Verbal fighting; arguing.

Jealousy? Hostility toward a rival or one who may have an advantage.

What's the difference between anger in general and outbursts of anger? Anger is the feeling you have when someone hurts or disappoints you. Outbursts of anger are demonstrations of anger in destructive ways, such as screaming or hitting.

Does anyone here know what a faction is? It's a group that exists for self-serving interests, and its members think of themselves as better than others outside the group.

What is slander? Saying something about someone that's not true and damages his or her reputation.

Arrogance? Being stuck-up or convinced you're better than others.

What is disorder—and why would it be included in this list? Students will probably know what disorder is, but it's doubtful that they know why it's in this verse. Paul is referring to the Corinthian church's problem with people shouting out and creating disorder within their worship services.

Continue: **So, here's the big question: Paul lists a bunch of pretty serious sins going on in the Corinthian church. Why do you think he considered gossip to be as serious as the other things listed?** The Bible makes it obvious in dozens of places that gossip is at odds with God's desires (see verses mentioned in Step Two: Option 1 of this session). It doesn't treat people with the respect that God's creation deserves; it's usually filled with inaccuracies and untruths; it's self-serving (used to build ourselves up at the expense of tearing someone else down); and it's destructive to relationships and community—both of which are God's goals for us.

Why do you think Christians are often just as bad about gossip as non-Christians? There's no one right answer here. Probably the biggest reason that we have a hard time confronting sin in others is that we enjoy it so much ourselves!

Read 2 Corinthians 12:20 aloud; then ask for a volunteer to read James 1:26. Discuss:

What does it mean to keep a "tight rein" on your tongue? Hold it back, not saying the first thing that comes to your mind.

How does James link the tongue and religion? If you bad-mouth others, your religion is worthless.

Do you think this is true?

Does that mean if you spread gossip and rumors that you're not a Christian? Since junior highers think so concretely (in black-and-white terms), point out that what makes a person a Christian is accepting Jesus as Savior and Lord. The "religion" that James refers to in 1:26 are the outward acts of religion, rather than the actual relationship with God through Christ. In other words, if you have loose lips, you minimize the significance and impact of your other Christian actions.

You'll need A cup of water, salt, a spoon and an inexpensive ruler for each student. **Optional:** If you'd like, this option can also be accompanied by a cow's tongue, which is big and gross and can be purchased at most local grocery stores. We've already suggested this in *Pulse 3: Friends* (Session 4, Step 1, Option 2, p. 56), but we thought it was such a great idea that we'd suggest it again!

The Big Idea

Your tongue is a small, but powerful tool that you need to control.

The Big Question

How do I control my tongue?

Read aloud James 3:1-12 and explain that this passage tells us a few important things we need to do about our tongue.

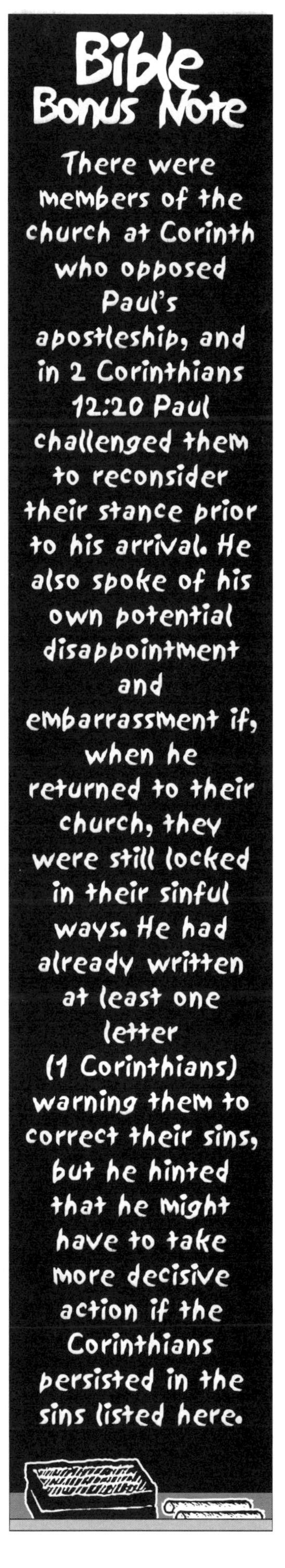

1. Recognize its power.

Measure the length of your own tongue with a ruler. Distribute rulers and let students (with the help of another student) measure their own tongue. You might even want to see who has the longest tongue in the room.

Explain: **Although your tongue is pretty small in comparison with the rest of your body, it has a lot of power because of the impact it can have on other people. The Bible says that the words we speak have the power to bring life or death to others** (see Proverbs 18:21). **Imagine this cup of water is your body, and I drop in just one-half spoonful of salt.** Ask for a brave volunteer to taste the water to see if the small amount of salt made a difference; then continue: **Our tongue is like the salt—it may be small, but it has a big effect.**

Pour more salt into the water, then ask someone else to taste it. Depending on how rowdy your group is, there may be a few (generally guys) who would want to taste it, but most won't. Explain: **No one who is honest would want to drink this water now. The reason is that too much salt has made the water undrinkable, just like too many careless words can poison our whole body. If we don't use our tongues right, if we don't control what we say, we will suffer the consequences. Like verse 12 says, we can't have salt water and fresh water at the same time. Too much abuse of the tongue really hurts us and those around us.**

2. Learn to control it.

Explain: **The good news is that the Bible says we *can* control this powerful tool and here's how:**

Listen before you speak. Read aloud Proverbs 18:13 and James 1:19 then explain: **A lot of tongue trouble could be saved by just listening to what is being said to you before responding back.**

Think before you speak. Read aloud Proverbs 10:19 and Ephesians 4:29 and explain: **Don't say everything that pops into your head. Choose what you say and consider what is better left unsaid. A good guide for deciding is to ask yourself *Will what I say help those around me or hurt them?* Say only what will *help* the person who's listening.**

This step helps students clarify what gossip is and isn't and to think through their own responses to gossip.

You'll need Copies of "Proverbs Gossip" (p. 64) and pens or pencils.

Divide students into groups of three or four; then distribute "Proverbs Gossip" and pens or pencils. Ask students to rewrite the verses in their own words. After each translation, they should also write an example of what this would look like.

Circle around the room to make sure students have a clue what they're doing. Allow a few minutes to complete the handout; then bring the whole group back together and talk through their answers and examples. Discuss what, if anything, the verses have in common (for example, all the verses show that gossip damages relationships), as well as what new insight each verse gives about the problem of gossip (for example, gossip not only betrays someone's trust, it separates relationships, causes strife, wounds deep inside, leads to arguments, etc.).

Have a three-minute time of silent reflection upon the painful consequences gossip can bring. Lead students in a closing prayer of repentance, asking for forgiveness and the Holy Spirit's help to choose their words with care and compassion.

You'll need Just this case study and some chatty students.

Here's a case study without an easy answer. We've provided some suggested answers in case students get stuck, but use the questions to stimulate discussion and don't let students off easy—encourage them to answer honestly and to defend their answers.

Rachel isn't quite sure where to begin. She has decided that she needs to stop gossiping so much. But her friends gossip all the time. And she loves it! She convinced one friend, April, to try an experiment and hang out for a whole day without gossiping. They forgot most of the time and gossiped like crazy. And when they remembered the experiment and didn't gossip, they felt like they didn't have anything to talk about and they got bored. Rachel's mom gossips all the time too.

Ask: **What options does Rachel have?** She could give up trying; change her friends; pray every day for strength to avoid gossip; and/or develop a support group to help one another not gossip.

What will help her break this pattern? She needs to replace gossiping with a more positive action or to immediately walk away when gossip begins.

How do you think her friends would respond if she stopped gossiping? She'd probably get mixed reactions. Some friends might actually start talking about *her*. But that's a chance she should be willing to take if she knows she's doing the right thing in the eyes of God.

Should she say anything to her mom? Yes. She knows gossiping is wrong and she should share how she feels about it. Who knows? Her mom might join her in her resolve to stop gossiping.

You'll need Just these real-life situations and their questions.

Read these case studies and ask students to decide whether the character is involved in gossip or not.

1. **I'm Gina. My friend told me she's thinking of running away, and I decided I should tell my parents. Is this gossip?** No, because you are truly acting for your friend's best interests. It is not gossip if it protects someone.

2. **Hi, Gina again. Now I want to tell my friends. Is this gossip?** Yeah, it's probably gossip because they aren't going to help your friend.

3. **Steven here. This guy in our youth group is drinking all the time, and I told everyone so they could pray for him. Is this gossip?** Probably. It's amazing how often Christians use the "prayer request excuse" for gossiping. You could ask for anonymous prayer by saying, "A person I know is drinking too much and I would like to pray that this person would stop before it's too late."

4. **It's me, Steve again. I also e-mailed Sam and asked him to pray for that guy I told you about. I didn't tell Sam why or what the guy is doing. Is this gossip?** Probably not, although if Sam knows the kid, you might just have asked Sam to pray for a friend of yours and been even more general. After all, God knows the details!

5. **Hey, I'm Christina. My friend called me and told me all these juicy stories about people in our school. But I haven't repeated them to anyone, and I don't even believe most of them. Is this gossip?** Yes! Just by listening to gossip, you've given those who gossip more power at your school. But if you tell them at the beginning that you don't want to hear the gossip, you might at least stop some of it.

This step helps students plan ways to stay away from gossip.

Note: Option 1 is the only stand-alone option in this step; Options 2 and 3 are continuations of Option 1.

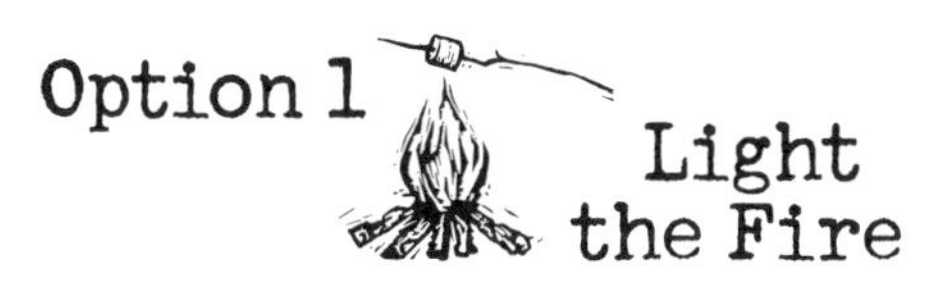

You'll need Several Bibles, 3x5-inch index cards (or half sheets of paper) and pens or pencils. **Optional:** Display the words of James 1:26 on a large piece of butcher paper, poster board or white board (or you can use an overhead projector).

Distribute Bibles, index cards and pens or pencils and ask students to think back about the past week and ask themselves, *When have I been involved in gossip during the past week?* (They don't need to write anything yet.) Now ask them to spend a minute silently praying that God would help them to avoid involvement in gossip.

Ask students to rewrite the verse from James 1:26 on their cards in their own words. Let them know that by doing this, each of them is making a commitment to God, so they should word the statement as strong as their commitments.

Invite anyone who would like to share what he or she wrote. Affirm their commitments and instruct students to keep their cards as a reminder of their desire to keep gossip out of their lives.

> **Note:** If using Option 2 in combination with this option, stop here and begin Option 2. If you choose not to combine the options, close in prayer, asking God to help students to be strong in the face of the temptation to gossip.

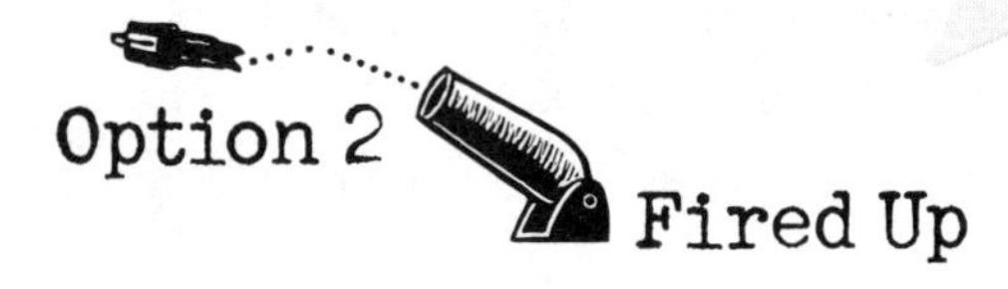

Option 2 Fired Up

You'll need The 3x5-inch cards used in Option 1 and pens or pencils.

> **Note:** Use this option as a follow-up to Option 1.

For students who are ready for serious action, take the last option one step further. Ask them each to turn their cards over and write the name of one person with whom they've gossiped in the past week. Then ask them to circle that person's name if they'd be willing to talk to him or her this week about their commitment to avoid gossip.

If students are willing to make this additional commitment, have them write a sentence or two saying how, when and where they'll speak with the person they've named on their cards and move on to Option 3 or close in prayer, asking God to open the hearts and minds of the people students listed on their cards that they might also be willing to make a commitment not to gossip.

Option 3 Spread the Fire

You'll need The 3x5-inch cards from Options 1 and 2 and pens or pencils.

> **Note:** This option is designed to be used *after* Options 1 and 2.

This option is a really gutsy act and you should set it up as a major challenge.

Ask students to find some blank space on their cards and write the name of someone they've gossiped *about* in the past week or two. Challenge them to go to that person and ask his or her forgiveness. (We told you it was a gutsy act!)

Explain: **This is a fantastic opportunity to witness to someone, because it gives you the opportunity to say "I really blew it, and I'm sorry. Just because I'm a Christian doesn't mean I don't do stupid things and I'm really sorry that I hurt you, whether you knew it or not."**

If students are willing to try this risky, extremely humbling step of faith, have them underline the name on their cards and write a sentence stating when and where they'll talk to that person.

Continue: **If someone comes to you with a juicy tidbit about someone else, what should you do? What words will you use to refuse to be a part of it?** Have students write a sentence they could say when presented with the chance to gossip. Close in prayer, asking God to give students strength to witness the truth to their friends.

Now comes the hard part for *you*! Remember to ask students in the weeks to come how they are doing in their pledges to avoid gossip. Commit to making your youth group a Gossip-Free Zone.

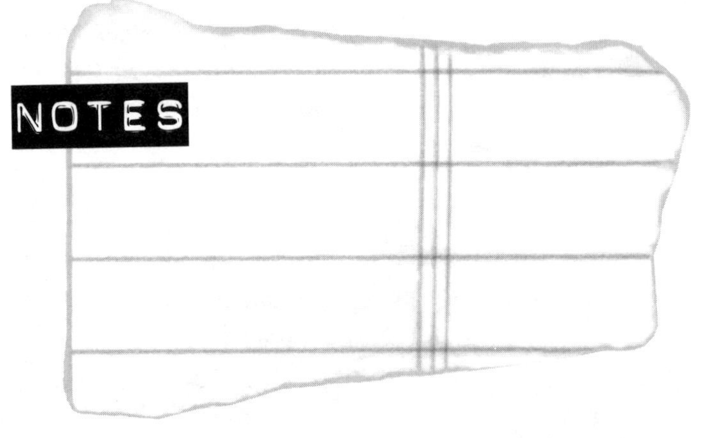

Rumor Slips

Rumor One
I heard that new kid is really weird: he doesn't have any toes.

Rumor Two
Hey, you know that new guy? I heard he's served time in prison.

Rumor Three
You won't believe what I heard about the new boy in class: he used to be a girl!

Rumor Four
I heard a fact about the new kid: he used to be superrich!

Rumor Five
You know that new guy in our school? He had to leave his last school because he burned it down.

Rumor Six
I heard something amazing about that new boy in class: he's on the run from the FBI!

Rumor Seven
Hey, you gotta hear this one: that new kid is really an alien.

Rumor Eight
I heard you should stay away from the new boy because he beats up people he doesn't like.

Proverbs Gossip

Rewrite each of these verses in your own words—words you would really use. Then write an example of what the verse means.

Proverbs 11:13
A gossip betrays a confidence, but a trustworthy man keeps a secret.

Translation:

Example:

Proverbs 16:28
A perverse man stirs up dissension, and a gossip separates close friends.

Translation:

Example:

Proverbs 18:8
The words of a gossip are like choice morsels; they go down to a man's inmost parts.

Translation:

Example:

Proverbs 20:19
A gossip betrays a confidence; so avoid a man who talks too much.

Translation:

Example:

Proverbs 26:20
Without wood a fire goes out; without gossip a quarrel dies down.

Translation:

Example:

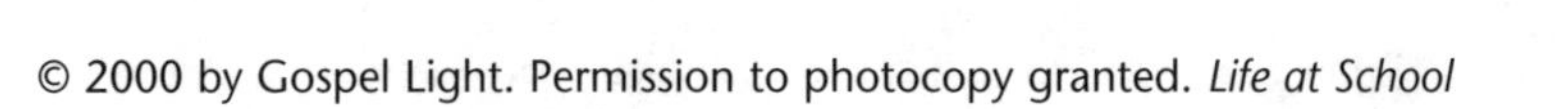

Quick QuesTions

If you wanT To avoid some pain, hobble over To Proverbs 25:18.

God Says

WhaT do you Think would hurT The mosT?

- ❑ Pulling ouT your fingernails
- ❑ GeTTing an arrow sTuck in your sTomach
- ❑ Having your hair pulled ouT of your head, one hair aT a Time
- ❑ GeTTing TooThpasTe in your eye (sTranger Things have been known To happen)

I Do

They all sound preTTy painful, don'T They? AlThough The Bible doesn'T Talk abouT TooThpasTe or pulling ouT your hair, iT does Talk abouT arrows. IT compares spreading some lies abouT someone To an arrow—and boy, can ThaT arrow do some damage!

Is There anybody you've hurT recenTly wiTh your words? Why don'T you go To ThaT person Today and leT him or her know you're sorry? IT's noT Too laTe.

FOLD HERE

Devotions in Motion

Week Four: Have You Heard?

FasT FacTs

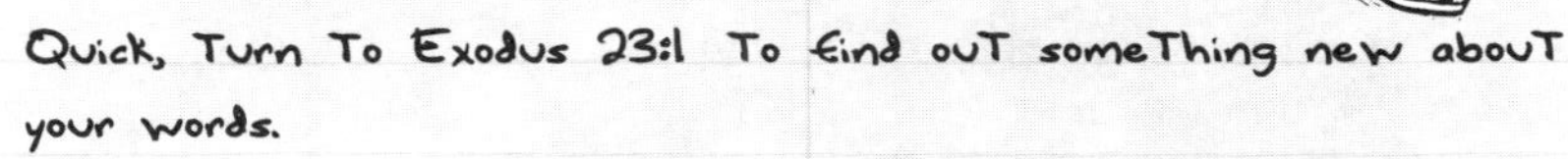

Quick, Turn To Exodus 23:1 To find ouT someThing new abouT your words.

God Says

IT sTarTed ouT preTTy simply. Dave Told Jeff ThaT Sam liked Kim; Then Jeff Told Danny. Danny misundersTood and Told Robby ThaT Sam had gone ouT wiTh Kim; Robby, Trying To make The sTory more inTeresTing, Told The resT of The guys on The soccer Team ThaT Sam had kissed Kim. Well, by The Time The news reached Kim's besT friend, Suzy, The sTory was ThaT Sam and Kim had slepT TogeTher. Suzy couldn'T believe iT. She wenT To Kim and asked if iT was True. Kim was shocked and angry; she couldn'T believe ThaT Sam would lie like ThaT!

I Do

Well, iT wasn'T Sam who had done The lying; iT had been everyone else involved. Some had lied on purpose, oThers To make The news more inTeresTing, and The resT had jusT misundersTood. Exodus 23:1 warns us To make sure we don'T spread anyThing false abouT oThers, so The nexT Time you hear someThing abouT someone else, The besT Thing To do is leT The news sTop wiTh you.

Quick Questions

Race on over to Proverbs 13:3.

God Says

Which would be the easiest to guard?

- ❑ The White House
- ❑ Buckingham Palace in London
- ❑ Your pet-rock collection
- ❑ Your lips

I Do

It's tough to say, but one thing is for sure: Your lips are something you have to guard every day. You can walk away from the White House, Buckingham Palace and your pet rock collection, but you can't turn away from your lips. You're stuck with them. And they can sure stick it to you if you're not careful.

How can you guard your lips today, making sure you don't let them run away from you and get you into trouble?

FOLD HERE

DAY 3

Fast Facts

Check out Matthew 12:34-37. Right here and right now.

God Says

"You are what you say." Rachel had heard the phrase "You are what you eat," but what her youth pastor was saying about Matthew 12:34 was new to her. When she got home, Rachel looked up the verse to make sure the youth pastor had been right. Sure enough, there it was! When Rachel thought about it, she realized that she had been saying some pretty mean things about the new guy at school. What did that say about her?

I Do

Think about the things that you have said about other people lately. What does that say about you?

Do you think it's true that our words are a reflection of what's going on inside of us? Jesus does.

SESSIONFIVESESSIONFIVESESSIONFIVE

The Big Idea

Your teachers aren't perfect, but God wants you to love them anyway.

Session Aims

In this session you will guide students to:

- Learn that teachers have lives and struggles outside the classroom;
- Express their feelings toward a particularly tough teacher at their school;
- Choose to respond the way God asks them to by not only showing respect, but also expressing God's love toward their teachers.

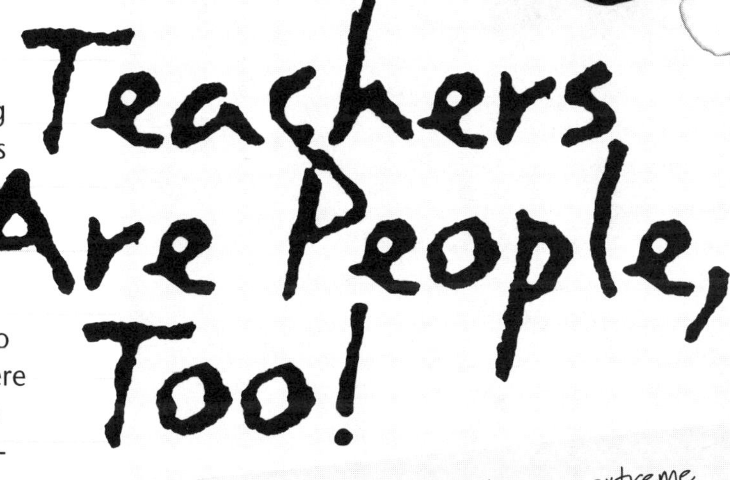

The Biggest Verse

"Everyone must submit himself to the governing authorities, for there is no authority except that which God has established. The authorities that exist have been established by God." Romans 13:1

Other Important Verses

1 Samuel 24; Jeremiah 29:11; John 3:16; Romans 8:28; 12:17-21; 13:1-5; 1 Corinthians 13:1-8; Ephesians 4:29; Philippians 2:3-8; Colossians 4:5,6; 1 Thessalonians 5:12,13; 1 Timothy 4:12,15,16; 5:1,2; 1 John 4:10

Note: This may seem like an extreme verse to emphasize, but how many times have you heard a student say something like, "My biology teacher has it in for me!" or "My math teacher hates me!" Even though most adults know that when teens say things like this they are probably being overly dramatic or sensitive, their feelings are still very real to them. So instead of telling teenagers that they're dumb to feel that way, this lesson teaches them how to deal with the situation the way God wants them to!

This step gets students thinking about their attitudes toward their schools and teachers.

You'll need Just this book.

Greet students and explain that you will read a list of commands that they are to follow. If a command calls for the students to move ahead or behind a certain number of seats and they're in the front or last row, they should move to the opposite side of the rows of chairs and continue playing from there. The same instructions apply if they're asked to move right or left and they're at the end of the row—they should head on down to the other side and keep moving! Don't take too long on any particular item—read through them quickly. There isn't a real winner or loser to this game; it's intended to get kids out of their seats and moving.

- **Stand up if you take gym class.**
- **Do three jumping jacks if you look forward to gym class every day.**
- **Move two plus two chairs to the right if you think you're good at math.**
- **Move eight divided by two chairs ahead if you know you stink at math.**
- **Raise your right hand if you can spell the word *receipt.*** Choose one student to spell it out loud, but don't tell him or her if the spelling is correct.
- **If you think that is the correct way to spell *receipt,* put your left arm in the air.** Now either give the correct spelling or affirm that the volunteer was correct.
- **If you were right, sit on the floor in front of your chair. If you were wrong, jog two laps around the room.** Move ahead with the game and let any joggers join in when they've finished their laps.
- **If lunch is your favorite time during the school day, stand up and turn in a circle five times, counting out loud.** If they don't count loudly or enthusiastically enough—make them do it again!
- Ask one of the twirling students to share his or her favorite school lunch menu item; then ask the group: **If this is also your favorite lunch, hop up and down on one foot 10 times—and count the hops so I can hear you!**
- **If you know the answer to this next question, look at the ceiling: Who was the president of the United States in 1862?** Again, choose one student with a raised head to answer (Abraham Lincoln).
- **If you think this answer is wrong, look at your shoes. If you think it is right, keep looking at the ceiling.** Once all the students have voted, share the correct answer and make the students who were wrong do 10 push-ups.
- **Hop from one foot to the other if you know the answer to this question: What is the normal body temperature of a human being?** Choose a student to respond, but *before* she shares her answer, tell the group that if she gets the answer right, everyone can sit down. However (aren't "howevers" fun?), if she gets the answer wrong, everyone must do 20 jumping jacks and then jog two laps around the room. Now get the volunteer's answer and follow through on the appropriate consequences. (The correct answer is 98.6 degrees Fahrenheit.)

Once students have returned to their seats and are settled down, discuss:

Were any of you afraid to answer a question because of the possible consequences? Yes, because I might be the only one who got it wrong and would be embarrassed.

Do you ever feel afraid to answer questions during a class at school? Most of us have at one time or another!

What makes you afraid?

How did you feel about that last question?

Do you think it was fair that one student's answer could affect the whole group?

Explain: **Well, although you're not usually twirling and running around your classroom at school, you do have to answer questions every day. Guess what? *So do your teachers.* And it's tiring for them, too. Today we're going to try to understand more of what it's like to be a teacher and how God would want us to treat our teachers.**

Option 2 Chat Room

You'll need A TV, a VCR and the video *Pleasantville.*

Ahead of time, cue the video approximately three minutes from the opening graphic to the three quick vignettes of teachers talking. (If you want to add some humor, start the video one minute earlier and play the clips of high school and the guy pretending to ask out the girl.)

Greet students and play the video clip; then discuss:

Do any of your teachers teach in such a negative way? (A simple show of hands here works fine; don't allow students to use the question as an open invitation to do any teacher bashing!)

These teachers didn't seem to care. Is that true with any of your teachers?

How would you describe your teachers?

Do any of you have a favorite teacher? Invite a few students to share who their favorite teacher is and then ask why they like this person so much.

Do you have a teacher that bugs you? Ask for a show of hands again and don't allow names—*that's* considered gossip!

What does that teacher do that's so annoying? Be prepared to only allow a few students to *briefly* share about their least favorite teacher. Remind them not to mention names. This could get long-winded if you let it.

Depending on what students have shared, be prepared to ask some follow-up questions such as:

Why do you think your teacher does that?

How do you feel when he or she does that?

How are you doing in this teacher's class? Do you like the subject?

Explain: **It's not easy to be a teacher and today we're going to see how we might be able to make our teachers' lives (and maybe our own lives) easier while obeying God at the same time.**

Option 3 Fun and Games

You'll need The following items for every 8 to 10 students: An adult volunteer, a flipchart, an easel, a felt-tip pen and a copy of "Course Concept Cards" (p. 77).

You'll also need A whistle, cow bell or something else for a signal that can be heard over the noise of teens shouting out their answers, and candy for the winning team (Little Smarties might be appropriate!).

Ahead of time, cut apart the handouts and stack a set of cards for each team in numerical order (with card number one on top).

Greet students and divide them into teams of 8 to 10. Provide each team with a flipchart and easel, a felt-tip pen and a set of concept cards.

Have the students line up a few feet away from their teams' flipcharts. An adult leader should be standing at each station to hold the stack of cards, to make sure the cards stay in their proper order, and also to make sure the students only see the top card.

Reminder

It is illegal to rent a video at the video store and show it to your youth group without first having purchased a license to do so. A blanket movie license can be bought by your church that will allow you to show virtually any movie to your youth group or congregation for one year by calling the Motion Picture Licensing Corporation at 1-800-462-8855.

Youth Leader Tip

Some of the phrases on these cards will be really tough for the students to draw and/or guess. That's OK! The frustration will help them (hopefully) relate to how teachers sometimes feel when they're trying to teach a class.

At your signal, the first player should run to his team's flipchart, look at the top concept card and start drawing so his team can try to guess the concept. The rules are simple: The person drawing cannot speak or gesture and no words or numbers can be written down until someone on his team yells it out. If a player can't figure out what to draw, he can pass his turn to the next player by running back and tagging her. Each team is only allowed two passes during the game.

When a team correctly guesses a concept, the adult leader holding its concept cards should award the team 10 points and wave so that you can sound the signal to end that round. At the sound of the signal, the player who is drawing must put down the marker, run back to her line and tag the next player for the next round. **Note:** If no team guesses the right answer after two or three minutes—sound the signal anyway. After all, the bell rings in school whether or not a teacher has fully explained a concept to his or her students!

After all eight rounds are finished, tally up the points and award a candy prize to the team with the most points. Instruct students to remain in their teams and sit down; then discuss:

Which concept was the hardest to draw?

How did you feel when it was your turn to draw?

How did you feel when you heard the signal to stop before your team guessed the answer?

How is this similar to what your teachers go through every day?

Explain: **Today we're going to check out what the Bible says about how we are to treat people at school, including our teachers. You just might be in for some surprises!**

This step helps students think about particular teachers and compare their attitudes and actions toward them with how the Bible says we should act.

You'll need Several Bibles.

Distribute Bibles and ask a volunteer to read Romans 13:1-5; then discuss:

Paul never says to obey government, but he does say "submit." What's the difference? Although Paul says we should respect those in authority, he was allowing for the possibility that the authority might be asking you to do something that goes against what God would want, in which case you do not need to obey. A good example of this is found in Acts 5:29, where the apostles were ordered to stop preaching the gospel but replied, "We must obey God rather than men!"

Explain: **We might often view teachers as enemies because they can make our lives difficult. One young man in the Old Testament who had to learn how to respond to someone who was in authority over him (but who was trying to destroy him) was David.**

Choose 10 volunteers to assist you in portraying the story of David and assign them the following roles: King Saul, a messenger, David, 3,000 men (three of the largest volunteers) and David's men (four volunteers).

In your best game-show announcer's voice, introduce the story:

> **Now sit back, relax and prepare to be wowed by today's scintillating story of a mad king named Saul, a friendship gone *really* bad and a future king on the run for his life!**
>
> **As you may remember from the Old Testament, a young lad named David was chosen by God to be king of Israel someday. But first he had a lot of growing up to do. David first met King Saul when he was asked to come play his harp for the king. And a short time later David killed a giant named Goliath who was terrorizing King Saul's great army with only a slingshot and a small stone!**
>
> **After that, Saul took a liking to David and asked him to come live in the royal palace. As David grew older and stronger, he helped the king's army defeat many of Israel's foes over and over and over again. Pretty soon there were songs being written about David and about how much better he was than the king. Well, old Saul became green with envy over David's many accomplishments, so he tried to hunt David down and kill him!**

Instruct the actors to begin their role-playing as you read 1 Samuel 24. They should act out whatever you are saying and repeat any spoken dialogue after you've read it. (For longer passages, they can just move their lips as you read.)

When the performance has ended and the thunderous applause has died down, discuss:

Was Saul David's enemy? No, not in David's eyes. Even though Saul was trying to harm him, David chose to think of Saul not as his enemy, but as his king.

What did David's buddies tell him to do? They encouraged David to kill Saul while there was an opportunity.

Why did David not take this opportunity to kill Saul? Verse 6 tells us that David respected Saul's God-given position as king and therefore refused to do anything to harm him.

How does David's story illustrate what Paul wrote about in Romans 13:1-5? Even when we have disagreements or struggles with those in authority over us, we can still choose to honor their position and seek to resolve the problems with respect.

What kinds of things do your teachers do that make it seem like they're against you? Assigning difficult homework, giving hard tests, requiring excellence in work, etc.

If David were to walk into this room and give you some advice about how to handle these things, what do you think he would say? God has placed teachers in authority over your lives to help direct and instruct you. When you choose to respect their positions of authority, He will bless you and cause you to succeed.

What might Paul say if he walked in this room to talk to you right now? All authority can be used by God to bring about good. However, sometimes that authority can be corrupt and expect you to do something you feel is wrong. Remember, the ultimate authority for our lives is God Himself. As you submit to His authority, He will help you relate to all the other figures of authority in your lives.

How is this advice different from how people at school, including you, usually tend to act? We are sometimes encouraged to fight authority rather than respectfully submit to it, just because we don't *like* what they're telling us to do. Yet, having people in authority over us is part of the order God has established. It was *His* idea. We should seek to follow those in authority, unless they're asking us to directly disobey God's Word.

To bring this idea home, suggest several situations when students must choose to submit to the authority over them, even though they may not like what they're being asked to do. Here are a few examples to get you going:

If a teacher assigns homework over the holiday break, do you blow it off because you don't like doing homework during vacation time or do you decide to keep a good attitude and do your best with the assignment?

If the principal decides to close down the lunchtime Bible club, do you stop meeting altogether and plot revenge or find another time and place to meet to pray and read God's Word?

Your teacher has decided that the class should stay in during break to clean up the mess they made doing a special project. Do you rebel and walk out as soon as the bell rings or do you give up a few minutes of your break to do what you've been asked?

The idea is to help students understand that submission is a choice they must make, and that most authorities in their lives are good for them in one way or another.

Option 2 Chat Room

You'll need Two sheets of construction paper or card stock for each student and a stack of magazines, scissors, glue sticks and markers for each group of five to six students to share.

> **Note:** This option might seem somewhat negative at first, especially in having students point out negative things about their teachers. *However,* use it in conjunction with Step 4, Option 1 (p. 75), and you'll see how these negative phrases become positive teaching tools!

Distribute two pieces of construction paper to each student; then divide the group into smaller groups of five to six. Distribute a set of magazines, scissors, glue sticks and markers to each group and ask students to look through the magazines to find pictures and words they can cut out to describe one favorite and one not-so-favorite teacher. Instruct them to create one collage for each teacher by gluing the images and words onto the two sheets of paper. Have them write a title (but *not* the teacher's name) for their creations across the top of each page. Allow about 10 minutes to work on both collages, reminding students that no vulgar or excessively cruel collages are acceptable. Wander around as the groups work and keep an eye out for any tasteless artwork.

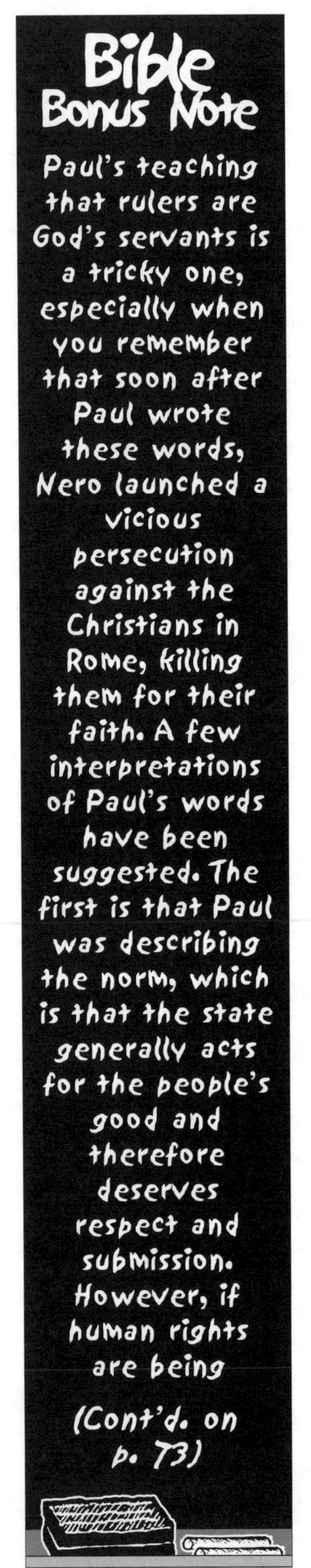

When time runs out, allow another five minutes for students to share within their groups what they've made and how each collage represents their teachers. (Before starting the next section, have volunteers gather up all the magazines and other supplies so students won't be subjected to the temptation to start gluing things to each other instead of paying attention to the rest of the lesson.)

Discuss:

What's similar about how you act around the teachers you like and the teachers you don't like?

What's different about your actions or attitude toward these two kinds of teachers?

Without opening the Bible, what does God say about how you are to act toward your teachers, regardless of how they act toward you?

Explain: **The Bible never talks about teachers in schools like we have now, but since teachers work for the government and are in authority over you, Romans 13:1-5 will help us see if your ideas were right or not.**

Paul never says to "obey" government, but he does say "submit." What do you think is the difference? Although Paul says we should respect those in authority, he was allowing for the possibility that the authority might be asking you to do something that goes against what God would want, in which case you do not need to obey.

According to these verses, who establishes authority? God.

How are our teachers "God's servant[s] to do you good?" They are trying to teach us things we need to know.

How do the reasons Paul gives to submit in Romans 13:5 relate to us at school? We might often view teachers as enemies because they can make our lives difficult. But the truth is that they are in authority over us to direct and instruct us for our own good. Most of them really want to see us succeed and become the best that we can be.

You'll need Your Bible, a white board and a dry-erase marker.

The Big Idea

Although teachers are an authority that we should respect, they can still be difficult at times.

The Big Question

How can we treat our teachers as God would want us to, even when it's difficult?

Begin by reading Romans 13:1-5, helping students understand that teachers are authorities over them and are paid by tax money, so Paul's teachings give some hints on how students are to treat them. The major idea you want to make sure students understand as you introduce this message is that teachers are God's servants. They are trying to help their students by giving them the tools to succeed in the present and future. However, that doesn't mean they're always easy to get along with.

1. Give your teachers the benefit of the doubt.

Remind students that teachers are real people who have their own set of problems, bad moods and bad-hair days. Share with them the saying that goes something like, "You can't judge a man until you've walked a mile in his shoes."

Now ask students to take off their shoes and throw them into a pile in the middle of the youth room. When you say, "Go!" they should go back to the pile; find a pair of shoes (matching or not); put them on their feet and return to their seats. Ask them how it feels to wear another person's shoes. Are the shoes they're wearing too tight? Are they a style they'd buy if they saw them in a store? Ask them to keep the shoes on their feet until the end of the meeting.

Explain: **Sometimes parents, friends—even our teachers—treat us badly and we immediately react in a negative way. But we don't always know what's behind their behavior. Maybe your teacher's car broke down on the way to school and she missed her first two classes because of it. Maybe he just lost a parent to cancer. Maybe he has a headache but had to come to school because the school couldn't find a substitute.**

Conclude: **Do you ever have a really awful day and you just can't help but take it out on your parents or friends? Before we assume a teacher is a jerk or hates us, we should try to give him or her the benefit of the doubt and try to understand what might be lying under the surface to make him or her act that way.**

2. Give your teachers a second chance by forgiving them.

Ask students to suggest things that teachers do that really annoy them and write these on the white board. Encourage them to leave the past behind and give their teachers a clean slate each day—just like God wipes our slates clean whenever we ask Him to forgive us. Invite students to come forward and erase whatever word or phrase really bugs them about their teachers, making sure that all the phrases get erased. Remind them that Ephesians 4:32 says, "Be kind and compassionate to one another, forgiving each other, just as in Christ God forgave you."

3. Give your teachers some divine assistance—pray for them.

Invite two volunteers forward, and explain that one is supposed to keep a straight face (no smiling), while the other one can do anything (except touching) to get the first one to smile. See how long it takes for the student to smile. If you have time, repeat this several times with different pairs of students.

Afterward, explain: **In this game it was hard to stay neutral, wasn't it? Did you know it's also hard to keep negative feelings about teachers if you pray for them?** It's true! Encourage students to take time to talk to God about how a teacher makes them mad or upset, then they ask Him to help them respond to that teacher in a respectful and loving way. Also, pray for specific needs and problems that a teacher might be having. It's almost impossible to stay mad at someone when you are praying for him or her.

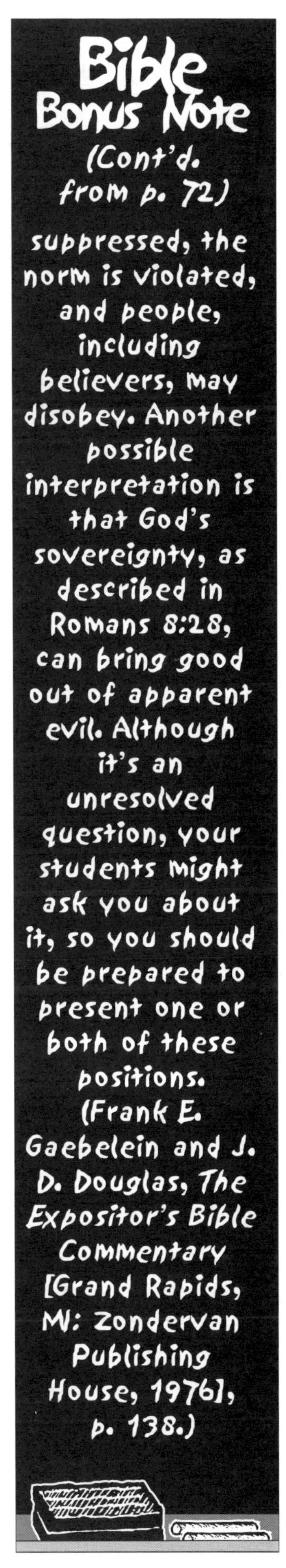

This step gives students some ideas for ways they can overcome their negative feelings and give their teachers the respect they deserve as people in authority over them.

You'll need Several Bibles, copies of "Teachers" (p. 78), pens or pencils and candy for prizes.

Divide students into groups of five to seven. Distribute "Teachers" and pens or pencils and allow groups several minutes to look up the Scripture passages and brainstorm ways they can apply each verse at school. Explain that it will benefit the group to come up with ideas that they don't think anybody else will and that the team that has the most creative ideas gets a candy prize.

After several minutes, ask one group to share its ideas. If any other group has that same idea, both (or all) of the groups have to cross it off their list. After the first group has shared all of its ideas, crossing out those ideas mentioned by other groups, ask another group to go, and so on, until all the ideas have been mentioned, and those written down by more than one group have been eliminated. Give a candy prize to the team that has the most unique ideas.

You'll need Just this here case study.

Read the following case study:

> **Erin sat down at her desk at the back of the classroom in English. She liked this class the most because she got to sit between her friends, Jessica and Andrea. Jessica leaned over to Erin and whispered, "Did you hear we have a sub in here for the rest of the semester?"**
>
> **"Yeah, Mrs. Stevens had her baby this weekend. She's on maternity leave," Andrea added.**
>
> **"Wow. Who's going to be our sub?" Erin asked.**
>
> **"I heard we're supposed to have old Mrs. MacIntosh. She was a sub in my science class, and she didn't like me at all!" Andrea said.**
>
> **"I heard she changes the seating chart so friends can't sit together," Jessica said.**
>
> **"I think I had her in history one time. She was kinda mean," Erin agreed.**
>
> **"Well, we'll show her. Brett has a plan to make Mrs. MacIntosh wish she'd never agreed to sub!" Andrea said with a chuckle.**
>
> **"What do you mean?" Erin asked.**
>
> **"You'll see. Just watch Brett and do whatever he does. If we all do it, then none of us can get in trouble. Right?" Andrea asked.**

Discuss:

What would you do if you were Erin?

If Brett's pranks seemed harmless, would you go along with the rest of the class?

What have you learned today that might help you make the best choice?

You'll need These questions and students who are up for a challenging discussion.

1. **What would you do if your teacher or coach asked you to do something you knew was wrong?** It's always best to do what God would want you to do. Tell your parents what's going on and get their help. Pray!

2. **What if you're doing your best, listening during class and showing the teacher respect, but he or she still treats you unfairly?** Keep doing your best and leave the situation in God's hands. Pray and ask God for patience and wisdom as to how to deal with this teacher—and pray for your teacher, too. If it really gets difficult, you may need to ask for help from your parents or school counselor.

3. **What do you do if your friends start calling you a teacher's pet once you start being nice to your teacher?** That might be a great time to explain why you're being nice to your teacher, using some of the reasons we've discussed today. You can also point out that there are some advantages of being nice to teachers, like the fact that you don't get in trouble as often and your citizenship grade is better than it was!

This step helps students change their perspectives about difficult teachers, brainstorm some ways to reach out to them, and then write a letter to hold themselves accountable to their new plans of action.

You'll need Pens or pencils.

Note: This option should be used in conjunction with Step 2, Option 2 (p. 71).

Have students take another look at the collage they made of their least favorite teachers during Step 2. Ask them to think of some positive words or phrases to replace the negative ones they glued to their papers. They should mark an X through each negative statement and write a positive one to replace it. For example, if they wrote, "yells at the class," they should cross it off and write something like "maintains order in the class" next to it. Remind them to try to put themselves in their teachers' shoes. This won't be easy for students to do (it's tough enough for adults), so ask available adult leaders to walk around and help students come up with some positive things to write. Allow five minutes or so; then close in prayer, asking God to help students view their teachers with His eyes.

You'll need Writing paper, business-sized envelopes and pens or pencils.

Distribute the paper, envelopes and pens or pencils and invite students to take a couple of minutes to write a letter to themselves. They should include three ways they plan to show their least favorite teachers more respect. If they're having trouble thinking of ideas, they can ask you or get suggestions from each other.

Allow a few minutes for letter writing; then have students place their letters in their envelopes, seal the envelopes and address them with their names and addresses. Collect the letters from the students and let them know you'll be mailing them out

Youth Leader Tip

As a youth leader, you are someone in a position of authority over the teens in your youth group. However, you have an advantage: They probably think you're way cooler than most of their school teachers! That's partly because you get to hang out with them and play cool games and it's partly because they can talk to you about God and other serious stuff going on in their lives. Oh yeah, and you don't give them grades that their parents eventually see. Students may not always thank you for the stuff you do, but deep down they do appreciate it. So show them a little appreciation in return. Catch them doing stuff right during your times together. Thank them for getting quiet the first time you ask. Tell them how you love it when they ask good questions. Give them a pat on the back when they listen to each other during small-group sharing times. If you take the time to really appreciate your students, they'll go the extra mile for you!

sometime in the coming weeks. (Make sure you do it!) When they receive them, the letters will serve as a reminder for students to continue to be respectful to their teachers.

You'll need A white board and a dry-erase marker. **Optional:** Construction paper, scissors, glue, glitter, markers, stickers, etc. and laminating paper or a laminating machine to create bookmarks or cards.

Explain: **It's one thing to show someone respect, but it's a totally different thing to show people God's love.** Ask students to brainstorm ways they could show one of their teachers that God loves him or her. Use the white board to write their suggestions. You can also use the following ideas:

Create a bookmark or card for the teacher with a word of encouragement and a Bible verse about God's love written on it. Provide some sample verses (for example Jeremiah 29:11, John 3:16, or 1 John 4:10) to get students started. This idea may not fly with the boys or even some of the older girls in your group, who may think they're too cool to make a bookmark or card. It's up to you to decide what will or won't work with your group.

Pool resources and buy little remembrances to give their teachers. Some items might be candy bars, flowers, pens, etc.

Write a letter of encouragement to their teachers. Students could point out something positive about each teacher's teaching styles or something unique about the class itself.

As a group, invite teachers to attend a special church event—an upcoming holiday concert, play or banquet. These types of events would be easier for students to promote than a church service.

Host a banquet to honor the teachers at a designated school. Students would use one school for the banquet and invite teachers from all of their schools. This would take a great deal of planning and adult help, but if you're willing to do it, it just might impact a lot of lives in your community!

Encourage students to think about specific ways they could show their teachers God's love and challenge them to do it soon! Making it a group project might get a better response. Keep a written record of chosen ideas and be sure to check back with students each week to find out what they've been doing to encourage their teachers. Have students share their stories. Hearing about their peers' successes will help others get the courage to act, too.

Wrap up by asking a few students to pray for the teachers in their schools, and pray that the students will show these adults in authority greater respect by showing them God's love.

NOTES

Course Concept Cards

1. History Class
In 1492 Columbus sailed the ocean blue.

2. Math Class
The square root of 16 is 4.

3. P.E. Class
Tackling is not allowed in flag football.

4. Lunch
Don't eat the tuna surprise!

5. English Class
I before *e* except after *c*.

6. Band
Whole notes are held for four beats.

7. Health Class
Colds are caused by a virus.

8. Science Class
Chlorophyll makes plants green.

Teachers

Brainstorm ideas on how to relate to your teachers based on the following verses:

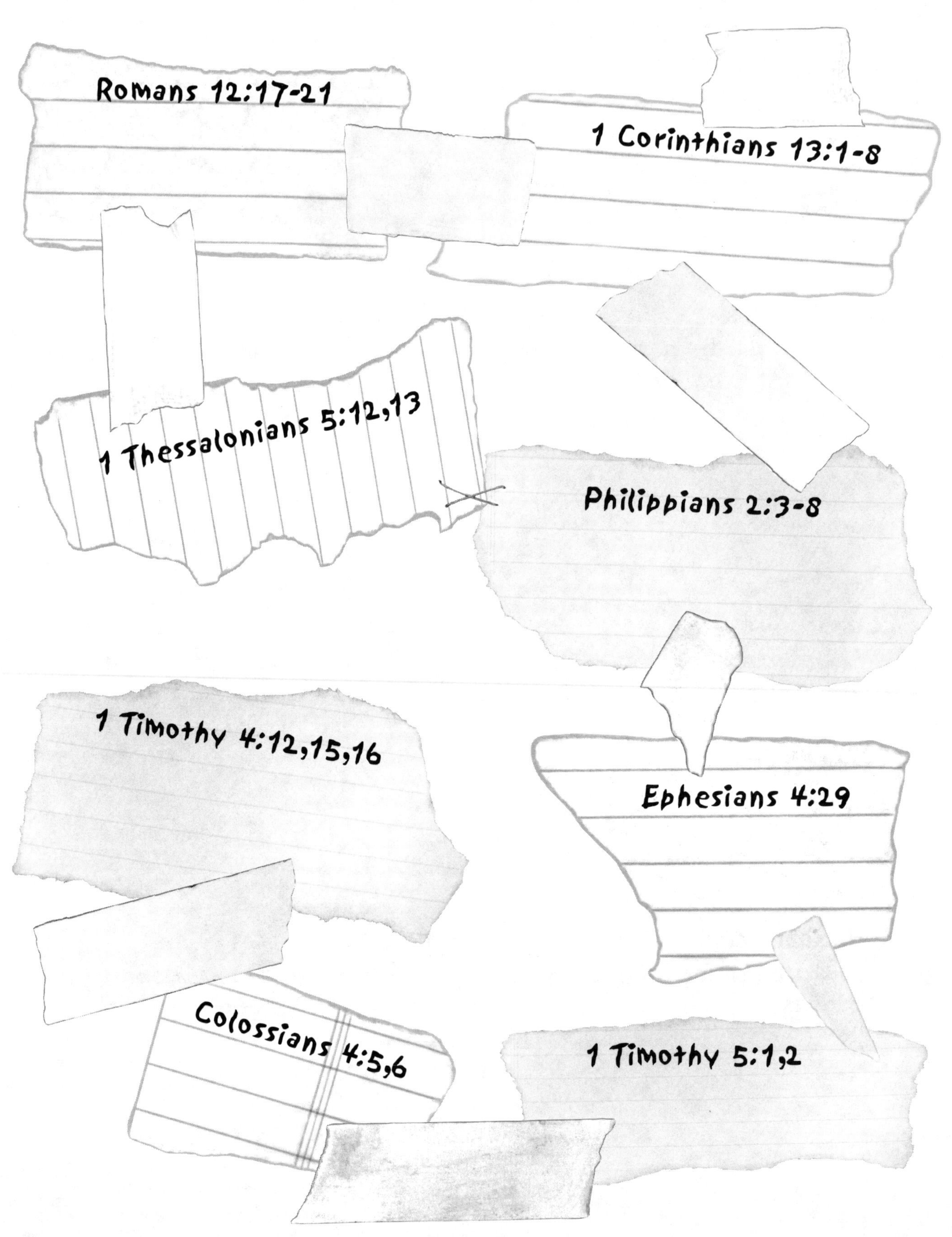

Devotions in Motion

Week Five: Teachers Are People, Too!

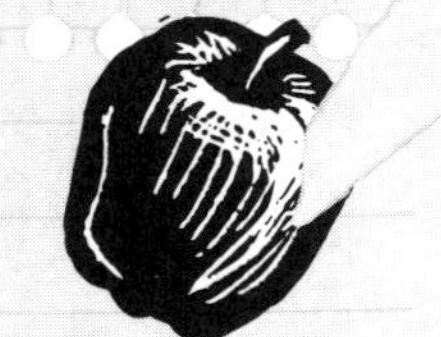

Fast Facts

Happy, happy, joy, joy! Go read Hebrews 13:17!

God Says

Jane Kindly was the science teacher at Fairly Middle School. Her job was a lot harder than it looked—she taught seven classes every day and never the same thing for more than one class! One period she taught chemistry; in another she taught about the solar system; and in the next class she would teach about the environment. She spent a lot of time preparing for each class, grading papers and thinking about her students.

Some of her classes were really fun to teach with respectful students who, even though they didn't know all the answers, tried hard to learn what she was teaching. Other classes were really hard for her to teach. The students were rude to her and spent a lot of time making smart remarks and pulling practical jokes. Often she was sad and tired at the end of the day.

I Do

Sometimes it's easy to forget that your teachers have a life beyond just being, well, teachers. They have friends, families, stresses, problems and lives just like anybody else. Do you help make your teacher's job a burden or a joy?

What's one thing you can do to help your teachers find joy in their work today?

FOLD HERE

Quick Questions

Hey, you! Yeah, you! Get to Proverbs 13:13 as quickly as you can.

God Says

Scott Hansen set off a stink bomb in Ms. Ivors's history class. Everyone ran out of the classroom and into the hall because of the smell, where they laughed and congratulated him. Ms. Ivors, however, didn't laugh. She sent Scott to the principal. At lunch, a few of the kids got together and talked about it. Which of their opinions do you agree with?

- ❑ "Scott was just trying to be funny! Ms. Ivors has, like, no sense of humor."
- ❑ "Stink bombs are gross; but it did get us out of class, so I guess it's OK."
- ❑ "Scott is totally immature, but Ms. Ivors is a jerk. It was just a joke."
- ❑ "That was totally uncool. I mean, Ms. Ivors has a job to do and Scott's goofing off is totally distracting."

I Do

Do you treat your teachers with respect?

Do you take the side of the class clowns when they disrupt class?

Do you talk about your teachers in a disrespectful way outside of class?

Is there anything you should change today about the way you treat your teachers?

Quick Questions

Hey, read Matthew 10:24,25. What do you think of yourself?

God Says

Imagine you're in Mr. Finkle's math class studying the equation pi when—blam!—you are suddenly able to read your classmates' minds! Which of these students do you believe has the best attitude?

- ❑ Jessica Platt: "This class is so boring. This teacher stinks. Why does he have to wear that stupid sweater all the time?"
- ❑ Henry James: "Pi. What a dumb name for a bunch of numbers. I bet he made it up. He would do something jerky like making up a stupid term like that."
- ❑ Tamar DeFoe: "Man, this stuff is kind of dry, but I'd better pay attention. He wouldn't spend all this time on it if it wasn't important."
- ❑ Kevin Ham: "Mmm . . . pie really sounds good. I wonder what my mom put in my lunch?"

I Do

Which student do your thoughts sound the most like?

Do you think your teachers have a lot to teach you or do you think you know it all already?

How respectful are you?

Do you need to change?

Pray that God will help you show more respect to your teachers today.

FOLD HERE

Fast Facts

Grab Proverbs 4:13 and don't let go!

God Says

Jess had trouble paying attention in her math class. It was her last class of the day and she always gazed out the window instead of listening to her teacher. Her homework and tests were full of red marks and she barely passed the class with a C-, but she didn't care. "After all," she told her friend Gina when school was finally out for the summer, "it's just a dumb math class. Who needs any of that junk anyway?"

Jess was really excited because she was going to science camp for the summer. She loved mixing chemicals together and looking through telescopes and all that stuff. Can you imagine how lost she felt when she couldn't figure how much of one chemical to mix with another or where Mars was in the night sky because she hadn't paid attention in her "dumb" math class?

I Do

Jess didn't think learning math was very important so she blew it off and didn't take the class or the instructor very seriously at all. It really caught up to her and made her regret how she had behaved.

Do you ever act like that or do you take your classes seriously? Pray that God will help you learn some new things today that will help you serve Him better (although you might not realize exactly how just now!).

SessionSixSessionSixSessionSixSessionSix

The Big Idea

Your school would be a different place if it were blanketed with love.

Session Aims

In this session you will guide students to:

- Learn the difference between exclusive and inclusive groups of friends;
- Think about reaching out and including outsiders into their friendship groups;
- Choose a way to show love to an outsider.

When Friendship Groups Get Ugly

The Biggest Verse

"Nobody should seek his own good, but the good of others."
1 Corinthians 10:24

Other Important Verses

Matthew 23:27; John 17:14-19; 1 Corinthians 10:24; 13:1-13; Philippians 2:1-11

This step helps students identify what a clique is.

You'll need A stopwatch (or a watch with a seconds indicator) and room for students to move around.

Greet students and select one volunteer (the Outsider) to stand with you while the remainder of the group stands shoulder-to-shoulder in a tight circle (for a group larger than 15 students, break into two circles or more). Ask the volunteer to stand near the circle; then when you say "Go," he or she should try to get to the center of the circle as the students forming the circle try to keep him or her out. Use the stopwatch to determine how long it takes for the Outsider to reach the inside of the circle. Repeat the exercise several times using a new Outsider to see who is the fastest at getting into the circle.

Introduce the session by explaining: **Sometimes there are groups that make it difficult to get into their inner circles. Today we're going to figure out how to respond to these kinds of groups at school.**

You'll need A TV, a VCR and a video of the movie *Clueless.*

Ahead of time, cue video approximately 22 minutes from the opening Paramount graphic to the scene in which three girls are walking through their campus, pointing out the different groups.

> **Note:** Further in the video, you'll find more commentary about a group that uses drugs on campus, which you may or may not find appropriate for your students.

Play the video clip; then discuss:

How does this scene remind you of your campus?

Is it a good idea to avoid certain groups on campus? Yes, some may be involved in harmful or even dangerous activities.

What is a clique? A group of friends, usually an exclusive group.

Where do you see cliques at school? Everywhere!

What part does popularity play in cliques? Actually, cliques are usually very fragile, and often one or two popular people define the whole group.

Are cliques good or bad? It depends on the type of clique. They are bad if they're exclusive—allowing only certain people who fit certain criteria (or rules of behavior) into the group. When people are excluded for superficial reasons, they will be hurt. Cliques are good if they are inclusive—allowing anyone to be a part of the group.

Conclude: **Today we're going to figure out how God wants us to act when we find ourselves surrounded by different cliques and maybe even belonging to one ourselves.**

You'll need One copy of "Cliques" (p. 88).

Ahead of time, cut apart the four clique descriptions. If you have more than 45 students, make additional copies of the handout. If you have less than 20 students use only two or three of the descriptions.

Greet students and divide them into groups of 8 to 10. Inform the groups that they are cliques and that everyone must stay within his or her assigned group.

> CAUTION
> Don't allow students to divide into real cliques of their own within their assigned groups. Try to break up the usual cliques for this exercise.

Give each of the groups a clique description and instruct them to spend a few minutes to understand their clique styles. Ask each group to provide two members that will work as a team to ask questions of other teams in order to guess the opposing clique's rules. Have each team come to the front of the room and give three minutes for each team to question one another. Award 100 points for every rule correctly identified (feel free to award partial credit if someone guesses close to a rule). The members of the clique being questioned must actively and fully answer all questions. Give bonus points to the team being questioned, depending on how well members play their parts.

After the questioning is over, reveal the rules of each clique; then discuss:

What kinds of cliques exist in your school?

What kinds of rules do the cliques at your school have? (For instance, certain cliques expect you to wear a certain style of clothing, talk a certain way or be involved in a certain school activity—or nonactivity.)

Who creates the rules in a clique? Sometimes it's the whole group, although there are usually one or two influential people in the group who decide most of the rules.

What happens when a group member violates the clique's rules? Usually, the person is kicked out of the clique or at least harassed until he or she conforms.

Transition to the next step by explaining: **Since most junior highers deal with cliques every day, let's look at what God has to say about them.**

This step guides students in understanding that God's love is God's greatest desire for how we should live our lives.

You'll need Several Bibles and one copy of "Act Up" (p. 89) for every four to six students.

Ahead of time, cut the handouts where indicated. Keep the different halves separate so that you'll know which half you're giving to each group.

Divide students into at least two teams of four to six students each (you'll need an even number of teams, so if you have more than 12 students, divide them accordingly). Distribute "Act Up," making sure to distribute the halves equally. One way is to give one type of handout to groups on one side of the room and the other to those on the opposite side of the room. Don't let on that teams have different instructions, but be sure to keep track of which team has which half of the handout.

Call the teams up "randomly" (but actually call up, one at a time, all the teams that have the first set of instructions) and ask them to follow the directions on the handout and perform an impromptu skit. Repeat the process for the teams with the other half of the handout.

After all these interesting performances are completed, ask if anyone noticed anything in particular about the skits: **Which skits were similar? Which were different?** You may need to give them a hint about comparing the first teams with the latter ones.

Read 1 Corinthians 10:24 and 13:1-13 aloud. Ask students to identify how these qualities were acted out in their skits. Ask students who received the top half of "Act Up" to comment on how they could have integrated ideas from these Scripture passages. The point here is that when we keep in mind what the Bible has to say about friends and cliques, we should act differently.

You'll need Several Bibles and a few romantic greeting cards.

Read the greeting cards aloud, making sure to emphasize any mushy-gushy language. Distribute Bibles as you explain: **There is a word in Greek for romantic love: *eros*. However, another word in Greek describes a different kind of love: *agape*. Agape describes the unconditional love that God has for us, meaning He loves us no matter what we do or say or believe—and He wants us to have that kind of love for others. It's described in detail by Paul in 1 Corinthians 13:1-13.**

Ask a volunteer to read 1 Corinthians 13:1-13; then discuss:

Why is love such a big deal to God? He can't *not* love—in fact, He *is* love!

How can you be part of a clique and still be loving to people? By not allowing the clique to exclude people or be mean to them.

Is it possible to be really popular and also practice what this passage talks about? It all depends on why you're popular. If you are popular for superficial reasons such as your looks, your athletic ability or your wealth, then your popularity is based on temporary things—things you could easily lose! But if you are popular because you love others with God's agape love, then you are putting this passage into practice.

Read 1 Corinthians 10:24; then discuss:

What does it mean to look out for the good of others? To watch out for other people's needs—to be kind to them, to care about their feelings.

Read Philippians 2:1-11; then discuss:

Who is our model for putting others' needs before our own? Jesus.

How did Jesus demonstrate that He put our needs before his? He gave up everything to be our servant; He gave His very life to save us.

Why is it so difficult to put others' needs before our own? We're selfish people and we are more concerned about ourselves than we are about others' needs and feelings.

You'll need Your Bible, a whole coconut, a whole orange and a straight pin.

The Big Idea

Each clique has a different feel to it.

The Big Question

What's the difference between a good clique and a bad clique?

1. Cliques can be bad.

Explain: **Anything that doesn't help other people is bad. 1 Corinthians 13:1-13 makes this completely clear: If you're the coolest person in the world but don't have love, you're worthless.** (That's a *very* loose paraphrase!) **This means that any group that's exclusive will be destructive to those who are excluded.**

To illustrate the concept of being exclusive, hold up the coconut and try to stick the pin into it. Continue: **A coconut has some really good stuff on the inside, but unless you can get through the outside, the inside is worthless.**

2. Cliques can be good.

Explain: **It's important to have a special group of friends. We all need friendships with people we can count on, but to avoid becoming an exclusive clique you need to be open to allowing others into your group. Try making up a new rule in your group of friends (your clique) that you'll include people into your own group that other groups might not.**

To illustrate the concept of being inclusive, hold up the orange and stick the pin into it. Continue: **An orange's outside allows easy access to the inside; together the good stuff on the inside and the penetrable outside work to make it inclusive!**

> **Option:** You might want to further illustrate the fun of including a variety of people by peeling the orange and sharing the (hopefully) sweet fruit inside, telling students that when they make an effort to get to know others, they just might experience the sweetness of a new refreshing friendship.

This step helps students wrestle with how to love others in their own lives.

> **Note:** Be mindful of students who might be the outcasts in the youth group or at their schools. Modify the following options as needed to include them in the discussion.

You'll need Paper, pens or pencils and a roomful of talkative students.

Help students think about their own groups of friends with the following discussion questions:

Think of one group of friends at school. Is it an *exclusive* group—closed to outsiders? You'd be hard-pressed to find a school that didn't have exclusive cliques!

Are the members of that group ever mean to other people?

Are there certain people in school that the group likes to tease or make fun of?

Have you ever been the victim of this type of teasing? How did it make you feel?

How might that group react if one of its members tried to make it more loving and *inclusive*—open to outsiders?

What about your own group of friends? Are they inclusive or exclusive?

Divide students into groups of four or five and distribute a piece of paper and a pen or pencil to each group. Give students two minutes to brainstorm ideas for making their friendship group (or their youth group!) more inclusive. Have the group with the most ideas share its list first; then have the other groups add anything that may have been missed. **Option:** Have each group choose its best idea and share it with the whole group; then ask students to vote on the idea they would use to include a newcomer into their own groups.

You'll need Just this case study.

Use the following case study to bridge the gap from thinking abstractly to thinking concretely on the subject of cliques:

> **Jenna really wants to be a loving person—just like the Bible teaches. And there are certainly lots of people in her school who could use a little love! But there's a little problem: Jenna has somehow been included in a popular clique.**
>
> **So, what's the big deal? The problem is that they're really mean to people outside of their clique. Jenna has tried to drop hints by saying things like, "We don't have to be so mean to people," but everyone just looks at her like she's an alien when she says things like that and they continue to treat outsiders badly.**

Discuss:

What options does Jenna have? She could drop out of the clique; she could continue to stick up for the ones being picked on and walk away when the teasing won't stop; she could make friends with the people who are being picked on.

What might be the cost of those options? She would no longer have an influence on the group; she might be ostracized from the group; she might become their next target.

What might be the reward? Knowing that she was modeling what God's love looks like.

Knowing the possible cost to herself, what should Jenna do? She should do what Jesus would do!

You'll need A Batmobile and a sidekick named Robin!

Bring students to a further understanding of God's expectations for how we should treat others by discussing:

1. **Why do some churches—who have God's teaching about loving others—seem to be the most unloving places on earth? Why are they so cliquish, making it difficult for "outsiders" to get in?** Christians are people too—and we often don't pay attention to this teaching of the Bible. This leads us to a sinful form of legalism, where we will only accept people whose behavior fits with the rules of our churches. Jesus called people like this (the Pharisees) "white-washed tombs" (Matthew 23:27) because they're all pretty and clean looking on the outside, but they are filled with death and decay on the inside.

2. **Why does it seem like so many Christians are the meanest people around?** Boy, if we could solve this problem, the whole world might want to follow Jesus! It seems the main difference, to oversimplify, is an issue of humility. If we focus on our sinfulness and God's grace, then we live a humble life of gratitude and will be more accepting of other people. But if we focus on right living and how good we are, we tend to get arrogant and mean.

3. **Is it OK to have only Christian friends?** Ooh, this is a touchy one! But the clear teaching of Scripture is that God never intended Christians to pull away from the world and live in their own little cliques. He wants us to not become like the world, but still we need to live in it and affect others with His love (see

John 17:14-19). We need to be loving to all people, not just other Christians. And you can't really love someone without knowing him or her!

Youth Leader Tip

Although this session helps students to understand the importance of being welcoming and inclusive, there are undoubtedly students in your ministry *right now* who feel excluded themselves. Face it: *Every* junior higher feels excluded at times. Remember your own adolescent years? Be sensitive to these students in your group and add a time of prayer for this issue at the close of the session. Have plenty of adults ready with open arms and listening ears.

This step helps students make a choice about how they'll make their friendship groups more loving.

You'll need Copies of "My Clique" (p. 90) and pens or pencils.

Distribute "My Clique" and pens or pencils and allow a couple of minutes for students to complete the handouts; then take a few more minutes to discuss their answers.

> CAUTION
>
> Don't ask students to share their answers for the first two questions on the handout. This could hurt someone in the room who's not listed or create more distraction as they think about that group. Instead, focus the sharing and discussion on the action steps.

After several students have shared, give students another minute to consider what others have shared and modify what they've written if they'd like to. Close in prayer, asking God to help students act on their ideas this week.

You'll need A bunch of 3x5-inch index cards and pens or pencils.

Distribute the index cards and pens or pencils. Ask students to think of a few people at their schools who seem unloved and excluded from groups. Have them write the initials of up to three of these people on their cards; then send them off on their own for a few minutes to pray for the students they've listed. Instruct them to think about these outsiders' loneliness at school and lift them up in prayer to God, asking Him for a specific idea on how they could show love to this person. Invite students to write on their cards any ideas that God brings to mind.

Gather everyone back together and ask students to put their names on their cards and give it to you if they're willing to try what they've written in the upcoming week. Find time during the week to contact the students who committed to doing something and encourage them in their efforts.

Close with prayer that students will find opportunities to reach out to outsiders during the coming weeks.

Option 3 Spread the Fire

You'll need A white board, a dry-erase marker, some creativity, time to plan and some *very* mature students who will take the task at hand seriously.

> **Note:** This activity is a wonderful evangelism/outreach tool. *However* (ya gotta love that word!), it's extremely important that the event is not viewed by students as one of taking pity on an unpopular student. Students must realize that Jesus reached out to the less popular, not because He felt sorry for them, but because He knew them and loved them. *Everyone* has something wonderful to offer others if given the opportunity. Encourage students to embrace the opportunity to reach out and make new friends with this activity. Let them know that the people they might invite will not be the only ones blessed!

Time to reach out! Youth groups can be the most exclusively cliquey groups on the face of the earth. Using the white board to keep track of ideas, have students brainstorm an event with the sole purpose of inviting students who aren't often included in other groups at school. The event could be as simple as a Friday game night or as complicated as a concert, but starting small is probably best if you have never done this sort of thing before. Once group members have caught the excitement, help them plan how they will invite others. Encourage each group member to bring at least one new person to the event, especially reaching out to those who appear lonely or left out. Have them plan how to make students feel welcome. Sell the idea to the group as a great way to make new friends and to show Jesus' love to others in their schools.

> **Note:** Delegate who is going to do what to make sure it all gets done. Be sure to follow up on each student or group of students responsible for a specific task. Some students will forget about 1.5 seconds after they agree to get something done.

NOTES

Cliques

Clique A: The Twitchies

Rule 1: You never speak without twitching your head to the right.

Rule 2: You speak very, very quietly.

Rule 3: You all love horses and can hardly say a sentence without commenting on a horse.

Rule 4: You can't stand it when people cross their arms—none of you ever do that. And when someone talking to you crosses his or her arms, you turn away from them.

Clique B: The Spazzes

Rule 1: You cannot keep still, ever. You are all in constant movement.

Rule 2: You speak loudly—very loudly.

Rule 3: You love M&M candies, and most of you are usually mumbling "M and M and M and M and M" constantly but quietly.

Rule 4: You can't stand it when people ask you questions. And when they do, you always roll your eyes and say, "If you must know," before you answer.

Clique C: The Snooties

Rule 1: You think you're better than everyone else and constantly look away with a stuck-up attitude.

Rule 2: You talk down to everyone like they're little children, and you all giggle when someone in your group does this well.

Rule 3: You love clothes and always ask people what brand they're wearing.

Rule 4: You can't stand it when people look at you. You regularly snap, "Stop looking at us!"

Clique D: The Grossies

Rule 1: You love to be gross—you burp and make rude noises all the time. (C'mon, get into it!)

Rule 2: You snicker and laugh at everything.

Rule 3: You love Jell-O and can't make it through a conversation without mentioning Jell-O.

Rule 4: You can't stand it when people don't talk. If someone just stands there, you start groaning and shout, "Aren't you going to say something?!"

Act Up

Come up with a drama sketch about what friendships and cliques are like at your school. Act out a scenario and conversation that would be likely to happen at your school. Everyone in your group must be involved, even if they are props or additional members of a crowd who simply nod their heads in agreement at times.

Act Up

Come up with a drama sketch about what friendships and cliques are like at your school. Act out a scenario and conversation that would be likely to happen at your school. Everyone in your group must be involved, even if they are props or additional members of a crowd who simply nod their heads in agreement at times.

In addition, you need to integrate elements of the following two Scripture passages:

Nobody should seek his own good, but the good of others. 1 Corinthians 10:24

If I speak in the tongues of men and of angels, but have not love, I am only a resounding gong or a clanging cymbal. If I have the gift of prophecy and can fathom all mysteries and all knowledge, and if I have a faith that can move mountains, but have not love, I am nothing. If I give all I possess to the poor and surrender my body to the flames, but have not love, I gain nothing.

Love is patient, love is kind. It does not envy, it does not boast, it is not proud. It is not rude, it is not self-seeking, it is not easily angered, it keeps no record of wrongs. Love does not delight in evil but rejoices with the truth. It always protects, always trusts, always hopes, always perseveres.

Love never fails. . . . And now these three remain: faith, hope and love. But the greatest of these is love. 1 Corinthians 13:1-13

My Clique

Think of one group of friends that you're a part of. Using only first names, who are the main people in this group?

Are there other people who are sometimes accepted in the group, but are not considered part of it? Using only first names, who are they?

Use the following scale to rate how exclusive or inclusive your group is:

1	2	3	4	5	6	7	8	9	10
Totally exclusive, no one can get in!			A little exclusive, it's not easy to get in			A little inclusive, we try to be kind			Totally inclusive, we accept and love anyone

Something I could do to get this group to be more loving to others:

Something I could do to make the group more inclusive (allowing a greater variety of people to be a part of the group):

Now, circle one of your last two answers that you're willing to do this week!

Devotions in Motion

Week Six: When Friendship Groups Get Ugly

Fast Facts

Who do you love? Read Leviticus 19:18 and find out who you should love.

God Says

Annie Dickenson and Lizzy Nuesbaum had been neighbors for as long as They could remember. When They were younger, They played TogeTher every day, buT as They grew up, They grew aparT. Now They're in junior high and Annie hangs ouT with The girls who are inTo drama and Lizzy hangs ouT with The skaTers. One day, Annie siTs down To The lunch Table and her friends are ripping Lizzy aparT! "She dresses like a boy, and Takes ThaT dumb skaTeboard everywhere!"

They giggled unTil They saw The look on Annie's face. She puT down her lunch and said, "Hey, jusT because she isn'T inTo The same sTuff you are, iT doesn'T mean she isn'T a cool person."

I Do

Loving your neighbor doesn'T jusT mean being nice To The person who lives nexT door. Your neighbor is everyone—The boy you siT across from on The bus, The girl who siTs in The back of your science class and even The guy who eaTs all by himself aT lunch. Are you loving all of your neighbors as yourself?

WhaT are Two ways you can show love To your neighbors Today in a way ThaT They wouldn'T expecT you To?

FOLD HERE

Quick QuesTions

Read Colossians 4:5,6 and be seT aparT!

God Says

Imagine you are aT The mall, waTching some people your age eaT lunch in The food courT. They're laughing, pushing each oTher, sTealing each oTher's french fries and being loud. You noTice ThaT one of The guys is cussing a loT and Two of The girls are gossiping and making fun of oThers from Their school. How would you feel if you found ouT . . .

- ❑ They were from your school?
- ❑ They were ChrisTians?
- ❑ They were in your group of friends?

I Do

How do you and your friends appear To people who don'T know you?

Would people know jusT from waTching you ThaT you love Jesus?

Do you seem differenT from oThers your age or do you acT jusT The same?

WhaT are Two Things you could do Today ThaT would make you differenT from oThers around you?

Quick Questions

What are you looking at? Go to 1 Samuel 16:6,7 and you might find out.

God Says

What kind of groups do you have at your school?

- ☐ Skaters
- ☐ Cheese lovers
- ☐ Geeks
- ☐ Jocks
- ☐ Actors
- ☐ Cheese haters
- ☐ Artsy people
- ☐ Rebels

I Do

What kind of group do you belong to?

How comfortable are you with people from other groups?

Do you judge by outward appearances or the condition of people's hearts?

Pray that God would help you see people as they really are, which is way more important than what they wear, what they do or how they look.

FOLD HERE

Fast Facts

Hey! Stop and read John 7:24 right now!

God Says

Ian was a cool guy. You could tell that just by looking at him! He had his nose pierced and his hair dyed blue. He wore gigantic blue jeans, T-shirts with the names of all his favorite bands on them, a hemp necklace and leather sandals. Ian knew he was cool and only talked to people who wore cool clothes like him.

One day in gym class (while wearing his dorky gym clothes), Ian met a really cool guy named Jack. They had a great conversation and Ian invited him to come to his youth group. After class, they changed into their street clothes. As Ian saw Jack changing into clothes that weren't as cool as his own, he realized how often he judged people by the clothes they wore.

I Do

Do you judge people by the clothes they wear or the activities they do or even the people they hang out with? You might be cutting yourself off from some great people! Just because someone doesn't fit the exact mold of what you think cool is, doesn't mean they aren't!

Be kind to everyone you make contact with today—who knows, maybe you'll make some new friends.

On the Move

How to Leave a Mark on Your School

Let's say you spend about 7 hours a day in school, 5 days a week. That's 35 hours per week. Then say you're in school approximately 40 weeks a year. Do the math and you'll find you're in school about 1,400 hours each school year! That's a lot of time spent in one place.

Now, don't get discouraged. Yes, that means a lot of teachers, books and tests—but it also means you have a tremendous opportunity to do something great for God. This thought may be new to you. You're probably used to thinking that school is about what you can get—soaking up everything you can learn before you get to the real world outside of school—not about what you can give. But school is a place you can give. You can leave a mark that will change lives (yours included!) and glorify God. Why? Jesus called His followers both "salt" and "light" (Matthew 5:13-16). He meant that they were to be the seasoning among the scrambled eggs of people, the ones that stood out and made the rest taste better. And they were to be the light shining in the darkness of a very dark world.

In the last few years, schools have become pretty scary places. Your friends, your classmates, even your teachers, desperately need you to be salt and light. They need you to show them the way to Jesus.

Step One: Develop Your Own Relationship with God

Light can't shine if it's under a barrel of sin; so in order to shine your light at school, first you need to have a growing relationship with Jesus. Don't try to be perfect; just love God with all you've got and all you are.

Step Two: Pray

Pray for your school, the administrators, the content taught in your classes, the faculty, your friends, classmates and other students. Find creative ways to pray. For instance, you could pray for one of the above each day of the week. You could pray using the days of the week—for example, pray for teachers and tests on Tuesday. (You'll have to be creative for those prayers that don't start with S, M, T, W or F!) Involve others in prayer and gather some friends to pray before school or during lunch. When people notice what you're doing, they may ask why you pray, and you'll have a great opportunity to share about Jesus. They may even ask to join you!

Step Three: Live So That People See Jesus in You

After Jesus' resurrection, Peter and John were arrested for preaching about Him. The rulers were amazed that uneducated fishermen were able to defend themselves with such courage. Acts 4:13 says, "They took note that these men had been with Jesus." Jesus so affected Peter and John that others saw Jesus' power shining through them. You can have the same effect on others around you.

Step Four: Treat People with Love

"Dear friends, since God so loved us, we also ought to love one another" (1 John 4:11). Jesus touched lost, lonely, hurting people. Jesus not only *said* that He loved the unlovable, but He *did* something about it. Try to imagine you're wearing "Jesus glasses" that allow you to see people the way Jesus does. Look for the outcasts. Look for people's needs and ask God how He wants you to love them. Making eye contact and offering a smile might be a good start. Or maybe you can help someone who's struggling in a class.

These steps may not sound revolutionary, but you don't have to start a campus club or stage a march (though you could!) to make an impact at school. Jesus started a revolution by loving and leading a small group of *ordinary* people. Following Jesus revolutionizes people's lives—if you point people to Him, He *will* make a difference at your school.